the technology, coordinator's handbook

Second Edition

Max Frazier

International Society for Technology in Education
EUGENE, OREGON ■ WASHINGTON, DC

the technology coordinator's handbook
Second Edition

Max Frazier

© 2012 International Society for Technology in Education
World rights reserved. No part of this book may be reproduced or transmitted in any form or by any means—electronic, mechanical, photocopying,
recording, or by any information storage or retrieval system—without
prior written permission from the publisher. Contact Permissions Editor:
www.iste.org/learn/publications/permissions-and-reprints.aspx;
permissions@iste.org; fax: 1.541.302.3780.

Director of Book Publishing: *Courtney Burkholder*
Acquisitions Editor: *Jeff V. Bolkan*
Production Editors: *Lynda Gansel, Tina Wells*
Production Coordinator: *Emily Reed*
Graphic Designer: *Signe Landin*
Copy Editor: *Diane Durrett*
Proofreader: *Ann Skaugset*
Cover Design, Book Design, and Production: *Kim McGovern*

Library of Congress Cataloging-in-Publication Data

Frazier, Max.
  The technology coordinator's handbook / Max Frazier. — 2nd ed.
    p. cm.
  Includes bibliographical references.
  ISBN 978-1-56484-319-7
  1. Educational technology. 2. Technology consultants. I. Title.
  LB1028.3.F725 2012
  371.33—dc23

                                                2012029037

Second Edition
ISBN: 978-1-56484-319-7
Printed in the United States of America

ISTE® is a registered trademark of the International Society for Technology in Education.

SUSTAINABLE FORESTRY INITIATIVE — Label applies to the text stock — Certified Sourcing — www.sfiprogram.org — SFI-00341

About ISTE

The International Society for Technology in Education (ISTE) is the trusted source for professional development, knowledge generation, advocacy, and leadership for innovation. ISTE is the premier membership association for educators and education leaders engaged in improving teaching and learning by advancing the effective use of technology in PK–12 and teacher education.

Home to ISTE's annual conference and exposition, the ISTE leadership conference, and the widely adopted NETS, ISTE represents more than 100,000 professionals worldwide. We support our members with information, networking opportunities, and guidance as they face the challenge of transforming education. To find out more about these and other ISTE initiatives, visit our website at www.iste.org.

As part of our mission, ISTE Book Publishing works with experienced educators to develop and produce practical resources for classroom teachers, teacher educators, and technology leaders. Every manuscript we select for publication is carefully peer-reviewed and professionally edited. We value your feedback on this book and other ISTE products. Email us at books@iste.org.

International Society for Technology in Education
Washington, DC, Office:
 1710 Rhode Island Ave. NW, Suite 900, Washington, DC 20036-3132
Eugene, Oregon, Office:
 180 West 8th Ave., Suite 300, Eugene, OR 97401-2916
Order Desk: 1.800.336.5191
Order Fax: 1.541.302.3778
Customer Service: orders@iste.org
Book Publishing: books@iste.org
Book Sales and Marketing: booksmarketing@iste.org
Web: www.iste.org

About the Author

Max Frazier has more than 30 years' experience working in Kansas schools. He has served as a middle school teacher, university instructor, educational technology specialist, and technology coordinator. He received a doctorate in educational administration and leadership at Kansas State University and is currently an associate professor in the School of Education at Newman University in Wichita. His interests include technology leadership, professional development, and working with preservice and inservice teachers to enhance teaching and learning with technology. He has been active in a variety of educational organizations at the state and national levels. He served as a board member with the Mid-America Association for Computers in Education.

Acknowledgments

I would like to thank Courtney Burkholder, Jeff Bolkan, and all the great people at ISTE for their support of this project and their work in preparation of this second edition. My wife Nancy has been a source of constant encouragement throughout the work on the manuscript. I also want to acknowledge the many friends and colleagues who have shared ideas, provided feedback, and given support as I worked on this project.

I must also recognize and offer my sincere gratitude to Dr. Jerry Bailey, my coauthor for the first edition of this book. His guidance and mentoring were essential to the development of the Technology Coordinator Issues Model and success of the original edition. Jerry has now retired from the demands of academic life. He is enjoying well-deserved time with his family and was not involved with the preparation of the second edition.

Contents

Contents

Chapter 3
End-User Support 63

Chapter 4
Network Operations 91

Chapter 5
Administrative Computing 121

Chapter 6
Planning and Budgeting 141

Appendix A
Sample Job Descriptions 171

Appendix B
Mini-Grant Application 193

Appendix C
National Educational Technology
Standards for Administrators (NETS•A) 197

Glossary 201
Bibliography 211

Preface to the Second Edition

Since the release of the first edition of this book in 2004, the challenges facing technology leaders have expanded and become more complex. The wide range of new tools and technology resources has created ongoing challenges for those who provide technology leadership and support. Given the continuous change facing technology leaders, an update to the Technology Coordinator Issues Model (TCIM) and the accompanying text is timely and appropriate. I have received a variety of positive feedback from readers, many of whom have made useful suggestions about issues to include in an update of this book. This second edition has given me an opportunity to address some of these issues and include information on topics such as Internet safety, the legal requirements of the Children's Internet Protection Act, 1-to-1 laptop initiatives, and student information systems. I am also pleased to include profiles of 10 technology leaders working in schools from Virginia to Hong Kong who support technology and student learning. The additions and refinements to this book were made to help the reader better understand the changing role of the technology coordinator.

Max Frazier
January 2012
Wichita, Kansas

Introduction

a position
without a protocol

The technology coordinator position is relatively new to K–12 schools. The position first appeared in the 1980s when schools began to use computers in day-to-day instruction (Moursund, 1992). As the number of computers rapidly increased, it became obvious to administrators that additional support was needed to manage this new educational technology. Funding a technology coordinator position was a first step toward creating the specialized support staff many larger schools and districts now require to assist with the implementation of both instructional technology in classrooms and administrative technology in school offices.

The number of technology coordinator positions in school districts increased dramatically during the 1990s in concert with the growing presence of computer technology in K–12 curricula. The National Center for Education Statistics reported that 86% of teachers had access to a tech coordinator at the district level (U.S. Department of Education National Center for Education Statistics, 2000). The number is even higher today. As the number and complexity of computers and networks increased during the 1990s, even small districts found it necessary to hire technology coordinators. These early coordinators were expected to provide technical and instructional assistance to teachers and students, plan for long-range integration and implementation of technology, supply professional development programs, prepare budgets, write grants, and even maintain the schools' equipment (Moursund, 1992).

Despite the fact that the number of technology coordinators has increased dramatically, there is often little consistency in titles and responsibilities among the positions. Lesisko (2005) surveyed 87 district technology coordinators in 24 Pennsylvania counties. He found 45 different position titles that represented a wide variety of professional preparations, educational backgrounds, and position expectations. These inconsistencies in preparations and expectations can lead to considerable differences in the way technology coordinators approach their everyday work, set goals for the organization, and make decisions. There is a need for a clearly defined and commonly shared definition of this important leadership position. A better and more consistent understanding of the position by the board of education, administration, and staff will help technology coordinators make better policy and budgetary decisions, and lead technology initiatives that are more reliable.

Although many school districts have added technology coordinator positions in recent years, the role of the technology coordinator often lacks clear definition in the district decision-making hierarchy (Miller & Brenner, 2002). Although the technology coordinator is expected to regularly guide technology implementation, technology staffers, principals, and district-level administrators often contribute to the decision-making process and influence choices.

Schools have invested billions of dollars in the past 20 years to purchase, install, and implement educational technology. However, the recession of 2008 forced school districts across the country to make budget cuts. These cuts have had a significant impact on technology investment as well as leadership and support positions. School administrators have been forced to delay purchases, reduce support staff size, and, in some cases, eliminate technology leadership positions. Although these decisions may have been necessary to meet the near-term budget requirements, the elimination of technology leadership and support positions, as well as regular investment in equipment replacement and upgrades, makes effective planning and support more difficult for the long term.

These cutbacks, combined with the ever-accelerating complexity of technology, have increased the demands placed on technology coordinators. Even so, few teacher training programs in the country focus specifically on preparing candidates to become school or district technology leaders. Currently, only a handful of states—including Pennsylvania, Wisconsin, Illinois, New York, and North Carolina—have established both academic standards for the training of technology coordinators and certification programs for those who aspire to work in this position. These states are only now in the process of training and certifying technology coordinators working at the district level. Most other states have yet to develop and implement programs to certify those working in this increasingly important position of district leadership.

ISTE has been instrumental in helping to establish standards at the national level for technology leaders and school administrators. The National Educational Technology Standards (NETS) for school administrators were originally released in 2002 and were updated and refreshed in 2009. ISTE, in conjunction with the National Council for Accreditation of Teacher Education (NCATE), has also developed standards for technology facilitators who work at the building or campus level, and separate standards for technology leaders who work at the district level. These standards are important guides for those who aspire to work as technology leaders and facilitators. ISTE launched a project to refresh these leadership standards at the 2010 ISTE conference and released the refreshed version at the 2011 ISTE conference. More information about the facilitation and leadership standards can be found in the NETS section of the ISTE website (iste.org/standards).

This handbook was developed specifically to address the need for leadership in this area and to assist those interested in serving as a school or district technology coordinator. With the help of this handbook, all stakeholders can more clearly understand the roles, requirements, and demands of a technology coordinator. Specifically, technology coordinators can use this handbook to be better prepared and have a fuller understanding of their position; and, in so doing, can be more effective learners and leaders, capable of assisting students, teachers, and staff in the use of these powerful tools. As well, education leaders can use this handbook to effect the institutional changes needed in order to make full use of the technology now available to K–12 schools.

Wearing Many Hats

In order to provide the necessary leadership in technology for a school or district, a technology coordinator will need to be comfortable wearing many hats. First and foremost, a technology coordinator must be able to establish and articulate a vision for the use of technology in a school or district, as well as develop a plan for successfully carrying out that vision. This must encompass a vision for (1) the development and implementation of appropriate technology policies; (2) the acquisition, monitoring, and maintenance of technology; (3) an effective professional development program; and (4) the provision of technical support for all end users.

The technology coordinator will need to employ a variety of skills to implement this vision. These skills include the ability to communicate effectively with various constituent groups, the ability to work with diverse groups and interests to effectively solve problems of differing types, and the ability to deal with technical issues that are always changing as the technology itself changes.

In addition, the technology coordinator must have the skills needed to carry out specific tasks such as:

- Communicating the organization's vision for technology
- Designing and conducting effective professional development programs and other training sessions for various audiences
- Developing appropriate and effective policies and establishing plans for both the short and long term
- Working with teachers and students to model the effective use of technology in learning
- Guiding purchasing decisions
- Assisting teachers with the effective integration of technology into the classroom

- Planning for and working with a variety of network structures and services

- Fulfilling the data and reporting needs of administrators

- Coordinating end user technical support

Teaching and learning are at the heart of all educational organizations, and they must be a primary focus of the technology coordinator. The coordinator will need to work with both teaching and administrative staff to select and purchase appropriate instructional technology resources for use in the classroom and then help teachers understand and use these new and exciting resources. The coordinator will be responsible for collecting and sharing information with staff regarding current research and best practices. By effectively managing these instructional technology tools and resources for the school or district, the technology coordinator can help to create a technology vision, aligned with the district mission, which can have a direct impact on student learning.

Providing end users with technical support is an important responsibility of the technology coordinator. Any organization that hopes to use technology successfully must be prepared to provide users of that technology with all the support and assistance necessary, working with them to diagnose and solve problems that can frustrate and compromise their ability to work. To help minimize user frustration, the technology coordinator must establish effective procedures for providing timely assistance and create a system for reporting, documenting, and repairing equipment.

The technology coordinator is also responsible for ensuring that software licenses and installations are current and that appropriate network and personal computer protection software is installed to defend against viruses, spam, and spyware. The technology coordinator must work with school or district administrators to create appropriate and timely plans for the regular upgrade and replacement of technology resources. By successfully addressing each of these issues, the coordinator can ensure that end users will be able to effectively take advantage of their school's or district's technology resources with a minimum of frustration and difficulty.

The school or district network plays a vital part in connecting class-rooms, offices, and support services for purposes of communication, data storage, and sharing of information. Consequently, the technology coordinator must be prepared to play a role in planning, implementing, and supporting network operations to ensure a school or district has the infrastructure necessary to achieve the goals of its technology plan. The technology coordinator works closely with network administrators to manage user accounts, maintain and support the district email system, provide Internet access, protect users from spam and intrusive software, and train users to use these technology resources appropriately. By successfully carrying out this role, the technology coordinator can help ensure that the network will operate smoothly and with a minimum amount of downtime, and that users will gain the maximum utility from available resources.

Another major role technology coordinators typically play is over-seeing the administrative computing operations of a school or district. A successful school organization must be able to plan, implement, and manage a variety of database structures to support management of student information and processing of grades, human resources information, purchasing and inventory records, and other informa-tion needed by management. The technology coordinator should be prepared to assist with the development of an information processing system that is both capable of handling these needs and is able to grow and expand to meet the future needs of the organization. In addition to planning and implementation, the technology coordinator will be expected to train and assist users of these systems to ensure that district employees can capably carry out the many tasks necessary to manage the business functions of the organization.

To be successful in any of these major roles, it is important that the technology coordinator be skilled in budgeting and planning. Because the technology coordinator typically has primary responsibility for developing and supervising the school's or district's technology plan and working with other district staff and administration to promote a shared vision for the use of technology, the technology coordinator must work with constituent groups to gain budgetary support for that vision and evaluate the success of the plan over time. The tech-nology coordinator is usually expected to help find supplemental resources, such as grants and E-Rate funding. By helping to establish and implement an effective technology plan—working with executive administration and the board of education to ensure the necessary budgetary support for the plan and securing supplemental funding for technology initiatives whenever possible—the technology coordinator can help ensure the most effective implementation of technology resources for teaching, learning, and business functions.

Organization of This Handbook

This handbook is organized around the Technology Coordinator Issues Model. This model was developed by the author of this second edition and Gerald Bailey. The model identifies the five main areas essential to schools and districts of all sizes that most technology coordinators must address (Figure I.1).

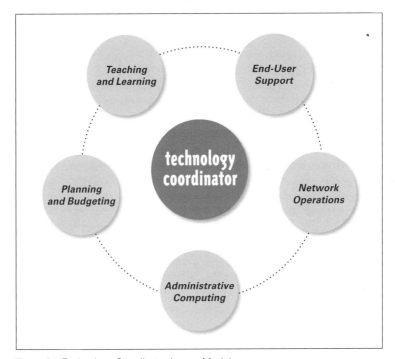

Figure I.1 Technology Coordinator Issues Model

The five areas identified in the model can be described as follows:

Teaching and Learning. The integration of technology into the classroom to enhance and enrich the learning process.

End-User Support. The ongoing support required by users of technology throughout the organization.

Network Operations. The infrastructure and equipment that make electronic communication and access to the Internet possible through local and wide area networks and other telecommunication services.

Administrative Computing. The technology software programs that support the administrative and business functions of the organization.

Planning and Budgeting. The planning and making of financial decisions required to carry out and support the school's or district's technology objectives.

Within each of these general areas, the technology coordinator must understand and address specific issues. In the chapters that follow, these issues will be discussed in detail, and their importance to the technology coordinator's overall responsibilities will be explained.

Additional Resources

In addition to the main text, each chapter contains a variety of resources that will prove useful to technology leaders and help them make effective decisions in their work. Sections appearing in every chapter include:

Essential Questions. Located at the start of each chapter, these essential questions are designed to help readers fully understand an issue and reach the best solution to a problem.

Answers to Essential Questions. These answers appear toward the end of each chapter and summarize the information discussed.

Tech Leader Profiles. New to this edition is a series of short profiles of educational technology leaders. These profiles provide snapshots of the leaders' backgrounds, their school or district, challenges they face in the position, and tips they have for others in leadership positions.

Resources. This section is divided into print and online resources. The books, journal articles, documents, and other printed reference materials in Print Resources are useful to anyone in a technology leadership position. Many of these resources were used in developing this handbook and will serve to deepen a technology coordinator's understanding of the field. The Online Resources include websites, downloadable documents, and other information found on the Internet. These resources can help you learn about new issues, accomplish important tasks, and stay abreast of new developments and techniques in the field of educational technology.

Boxed items with additional information include:

Helpful Hints. These useful ideas will help the technology coordinator deal with difficult problems and tricky situations likely faced on the job.

Toolbox Tips. Toolbox Tips are concrete recommendations for dealing with specific issues or situations. These techniques are currently used by technology coordinators in the field or are derived from resources in the literature.

Useful forms and samples can be found throughout the book. For quick reference, consult the table of contents and locate the entries that appear in italic type.

Appendix A provides sample job descriptions, Appendix B is a mini-grant application form and budget, and Appendix C contains the National Educational Technology Standards for Administrators (NETS•A). This handbook also provides a glossary of key terms (glossary terms appear in **bold italic type** in the text) and a bibliography.

A Guide and a Reference

This handbook is intended to serve as a useful guide and reference. It is designed to be used in a variety of different ways: as a guide for understanding essential questions, as a reference for finding useful information, and as a model for identifying the wide variety of tasks and responsibilities faced by technology coordinators.

This handbook can be read from beginning to end, but it can also be used as a reference tool and accessed as needed to find information on a particular area of interest. Skimming the entire handbook should provide an overview of the issues and responsibilities that make up the technology coordinator position. An in-depth reading of a single chapter should provide sufficient background on a particular area of responsibility, such as computer support.

The handbook should also be useful in helping district administrators and board of education members understand the wide range of technology issues and questions that must be addressed to successfully use technology and integrate it into the educational process and other school district operations. Those who do not provide technological support and leadership on a daily basis may lack the in-depth understanding of the technology coordinator. The figures, examples, references, and resources of this handbook should be useful in helping them understand and address the complex issues of technology implementation.

One goal of this handbook is to help focus the discussion in the United States regarding certification standards for the technology coordinator. While this handbook cannot be viewed as a comprehensive document that addresses all issues faced by technology coordinators, it nonetheless provides an important and useful description of the work performed by the technology coordinator, and serves as a functional reference for those who aspire to, or currently serve in, this important technological leadership position. We hope this handbook can serve as a point of departure in the discussion of the important issues, and how they should be addressed, in order to provide effective technological leadership for a school organization.

chapter 1

district organization

Essential Questions

1. What are the major responsibilities the technology coordinator will be expected to assume?

2. What skills and abilities will be needed to succeed in the position?

3. What day-to-day operational tasks will the technology coordinator most likely face?

4. What qualifications and job requirements are typically expected of technology coordinators?

5. What type of leadership role will the technology coordinator play in the school or district?

Basic Responsibilities

The technology coordinator plays a vital role in the leadership of a school or district. This individual must be prepared to assist in directing and supporting all aspects of technology use, from instructional and technical support to **network** operations, **administrative computing,** and budgeting and planning.

The demands of this position require that technology coordinators have a variety of skills and talents in order to be successful in their many duties (Jewell, 1999). Technology coordinators may, and probably will, serve as technicians, trainers, curriculum consultants, curriculum designers, planners, and policy makers (Marcovitz, 1998). They need to have a clear understanding of how a school's or district's technology resources are being used by teachers and students, office workers, administrators, and network technicians. While the technology coordinator cannot be expected to have specific expertise in all of these areas, a general understanding of each is essential for success in this position.

Moursund (1992) defined four broad skill sets for successful technology coordinators:

- A broad general education and dedication to lifelong learning
- Knowledge of and support for the educational system
- Good skills in interpersonal relationships
- Adequate technical knowledge

It is important to note that three of these four areas are not technology-related at all, and yet they are still necessary to be successful in the position. The technology coordinator will work with a wide variety of people and must be committed to serving a diverse community of technology users with many different priorities.

The ideal person to serve as a technology coordinator may be a hybrid of educator and technician (Bushweller, 1996). Such a person has the computer skills necessary to satisfy the technical requirements of the position and experience as an educator, which is invaluable for understanding and serving technology users in a school setting.

Technology coordinators must be familiar with the many types of equipment and the variety of *software* programs used by teachers and students in the classroom (Durost, 1994). Typical classroom programs include general software tools such as word processors, *spreadsheets, database* programs, *web browsers,* and *email clients,* as well as specialized tools such as online encyclopedias, library catalog programs, and grade book programs.

Experience as a teacher in a classroom setting is often useful in understanding the demands of working with students. This experience, along with knowledge of the adult learning process, can be very helpful in conducting *professional development* and training activities for teachers and other staff members, which is one of the primary responsibilities for most technology coordinators.

Technology users frequently need assistance in a variety of different areas, from hardware support to assistance with software or online resources. These users will expect the technology coordinator to be knowledgeable in every area and will look to them for any needed support. The support of classroom computers will often require *troubleshooting* both hardware and software problems. Although direct responsibility for maintenance and repair of equipment may fall to someone else, the tech coordinator will often be found assisting in the resolution of technical problems by diagnosing and solving difficulties with equipment (Jewell, 1999).

Technology coordinators must also have at least a basic understanding of the organization and operation of a school's or district's computer network. Management and maintenance of *servers* and network equipment are highly technical in nature and require specialized training. In most large school districts today these tasks are performed by certified network administrators. However, the technology coordinator should still be prepared to address basic issues and problems related to network connectivity and server capacity in order to support users, plan for appropriate *infrastructure,* and manage budgets.

School and district administrators and office staff rely on technology to manage student information and business operations. The technology coordinator must therefore possess a good understanding of the *information management* and *data processing* needs of the organization. In a large school district, these systems may be quite complex and involve specialized programming and data processing skills that are regularly handled by other members of the technology staff. The technology coordinator, however, must understand these systems well enough to know how to optimize the school's or district's existing technology infrastructure in order to meet the needs of these particular users.

The technology coordinator's major responsibilities, then, all revolve around a single objective: to ensure that a school's or district's technology resources are being used as effectively as possible by all members of the organization—teachers, students, administrators, and staff. It is important for technology coordinators to keep this goal in mind when dealing with the widely variant, day-to-day pressures of the job.

Important decisions regarding technology should always be based on careful research and planning, and final design choices should be both manageable and feasible. Without proper information, poor decisions and costly mistakes can be made. A major role of the technology coordinator is to gather and maintain the essential information required for good decision making. The technology coordinator must be able to determine and articulate how technology will be used organization-wide, and then use this information to make effective decisions and communicate them to administrators, teachers, and other district staff (Jewell, 1999).

Essential Skills and Qualifications

Certain skills are necessary in order to be successful as a technology coordinator. One of the most important is a good understanding of the role of the teacher in the educational process, preferably from actual classroom experience as a teacher. The technology coordinator benefits from being able to see things from a teacher's perspective. This perspective helps the technology coordinator to effectively support and advocate for technology integration in the classroom.

Although not all schools have chosen an experienced educator as their technology coordinator, those who have selected noneducators have sometimes found limitations in what they can do (Bushweller, 1996). This position does require certain technical skills, and as *educational technology* becomes ever more complex, a technical background will become increasingly valuable. However, technology coordinators typically spend more time teaching people how to use technology than they do working with the hardware and software itself. For example, technology coordinators are often responsible for designing and implementing technology professional development instruction for teachers and staff members. Because the technology coordinator must constantly evaluate the comfort level of teachers and design the instruction appropriately, they must have good interpersonal and communication skills. Coordinators must find multiple ways to promote technology competency and help teachers take the required risks necessary to effectively implement technology in their classrooms (Hoffman, 1996), and those who understand what teachers go through on a day-to-day basis will likely be far more successful at it.

Teaching experience is also useful for technology coordinators because it helps them conceptualize how technology can be effectively integrated into a classroom setting to enhance learning. A coordinator who is able to demonstrate a practical understanding of classroom dynamics and basic pedagogy has a much greater chance of convincing teachers that technology integration is both desirable and doable.

Other essential qualifications for technology coordinators include strong skills in leadership, organization, and communication. Because a great deal of their work involves gathering, synthesizing, and disseminating a wealth of information about technology, coordinators must be both highly analytic and personable. On any given day, they will need to work with a wide variety of people at many different skill levels, both inside and outside the organization—students, teachers, administrators, kitchen staff, board of education members, community representatives, vendors, and so forth. Technology coordinators need solid writing skills to compose effective and persuasive reports, web pages, support emails, policies, and handouts. Strong telephone and speaking skills are vital, too. Knowledge of and experience with community relations can be very useful, because coordinators often help schools promote technology through events such as "technology night" and through presentations to the board of education and other community groups. Working with diverse groups and communicating effectively in a variety of ways are a major part of the day-to-day work of a technology coordinator.

Although it is important to recognize the nontechnical skills that technology coordinators must bring to their work, it is undeniable that technical qualifications are important as well. In addition to proficiency in diagnosing and solving problems with hardware and software, coordinators should be knowledgeable about trends and new developments in the field of educational technology. Although the technology coordinator may not be directly responsible for solving all technical problems, familiarity with a school's or district's technology resources and the ability to diagnose and solve general problems as they arise are essential.

Finally, technology coordinators need to possess planning, budgeting, and information management skills. **Technology plans** must be developed, implemented, and updated on a regular basis. Budgets for the purchase and maintenance of technology resources must be matched to the needs of the school or district, and then carefully managed. Inventories of district equipment and materials must be gathered, stored, and updated on a regular basis.

Needless to say, the ideal technology coordinator would have qualifications that range from network management to teacher education to public relations. No individual is likely to possess all these skills when beginning in the position; rather, these skills are developed over time. Perhaps a technology coordintator's most useful skill is a lifelong dedication to learning. The technology coordinator is constantly faced with learning new things, adapting to new situations, and researching techniques and equipment on the leading edge. The ability to learn and adapt to myriad situations serves the technology coordinator well.

Sample Job Description

Job descriptions for a technology coordinator position vary widely depending on the needs of a particular organization and the technological savvy of administrators. Some technology coordinators have emerged from the business world with MBAs and impressive technical experiences, but without any formal training in education (Bushweller, 1996). Others started out as teachers and entered their positions with little formal training, minimal administrative support, and, at times, no real job description (Jewell, 1999).

The job description for the technology coordinator of a small rural district may be quite different from that for a large urban or suburban district. A coordinator in a small district may be responsible for doing all technology-related tasks—from planning and troubleshooting to training and budgeting. In a larger organization, a professional staff may maintain the network and servers and offer hardware support, which then allows the technology coordinator to concentrate on professional development and the integration of technology into the curriculum. Whatever the size of the organization, however, it is important that the technology coordinator job description accurately describe the expectations, qualifications, and responsibilities of the position.

The following job description offers some generally accepted ideas about what schools and districts are looking for in applicants for technology coordinator positions. This generic description was compiled from a variety of job descriptions posted by districts across the nation. While these districts were diverse in their needs and requirements, common elements have been combined to identify the essential skills, duties, and responsibilities typically expected of this position. This description can serve as an example of how the position may be described on a job notice board, and it can be used as a model for developing a more specific description that aligns with the needs of a particular organization. See Appendix A for more examples.

sample job description

POSITION TITLE

District Technology Coordinator

JOB GOAL

Serves as the technology coordinator to plan, develop, implement, evaluate, and maintain an exemplary first-class technology program for the district. This will include support for students, teachers, support staff, and administrative staff.

ESSENTIAL DUTIES AND RESPONSIBILITIES

- Provide visionary leadership and articulate that vision in areas of responsibility.
- Build working relationships with key community leaders and organizations.
- Develop plans to increase the level of technological literacy for students, faculty, and staff.
- Assist the district in developing and implementing an educational technology infrastructure that meets system-wide needs.
- Provide leadership in technology training, resources acquisition, and professional development.
- Design, coordinate, and provide educational technology inservice opportunities for school-based personnel.
- Administer and manage the district intranet for sharing information internally with staff, and develop pages and information to be placed on the public website.
- Assist educators in using and integrating technology in the instructional program.
- Model effective uses of appropriate instructional technology in the classroom and the school media center.

sample job description (continued)

- Support teacher and student use of computers in classrooms.

- Provide staff with information about technology developments in their specific area of responsibility.

- Provide day-to-day management of technology department personnel such as network administrators, PC technicians, help desk operators, and others who work to support technology operations.

- Develop a system-wide technology plan, evaluate it annually, and modify it as needed.

- Recommend budget requirements to effectively support the district technology plan.

- Prepare and present reports on technology issues as directed by the superintendent and board of education.

ESSENTIAL SKILLS AND QUALIFICATIONS

- Master's degree in technology, education, or related field.

- Knowledge and understanding of the field of educational technology.

- Successful experience in the use of technology in a K–12 school district.

- Demonstrated ability to work with people as part of a team.

- Leadership and organizational skills.

- Ability to effectively relate to students, teachers, and other staff.

SALARY RANGE

$40,000 to $60,000 (*Authors' Note:* The salary will be dependent on experience, specific responsibilities, and the size of the district. The most common range should be $40,000 to $60,000. For a very large district, the salary range may be as high as $70,000 to $90,000.)

The Technology Coordinator Issues Model

In most schools and districts, the technology coordinator serves in a leadership position within the organizational structure. However, technology coordinators are often hired and work under the negotiated agreement as a teacher leader rather than as a district administrator; in other words, though they have a title and hold a position of responsibility, they may not actually be an administrator. Many districts have preferred to keep the technology coordinator as part of the teaching staff, even though the coordinator may have supervisory responsibilities and work with adults rather than children. The actual job title varies considerably from district to district—from "coordinator" to "director" to "specialist." Regardless of the title, though, the responsibilities and issues that people in this position typically face are usually quite similar.

The technology coordinator is the person who blazes a trail for technology in the school or district and understands how all the hardware, software, policies, and procedures fit together in the big picture of a school's or district's technology implementation (Jewell, 1999). The tech coordinator should be prepared to help teachers, staff, administrators, and board of education members use technology more effectively and meet the standards and goals laid out in the district's technology plan. The coordinator must find and accumulate adequate funding and administrative support to make a school's or district's technology initiatives feasible, as well as budget successfully for the necessary resources for installation, maintenance, and training (Ritchie, 1996).

The Technology Coordinator Issues Model (TCIM) in Figure 1.1 is intended to provide a complete overview of the various areas of responsibility that comprise the technology coordinator position. The model articulates several specific issues within each general area that most technology coordinators must address to effectively support and integrate technology use in all aspects of the organization.

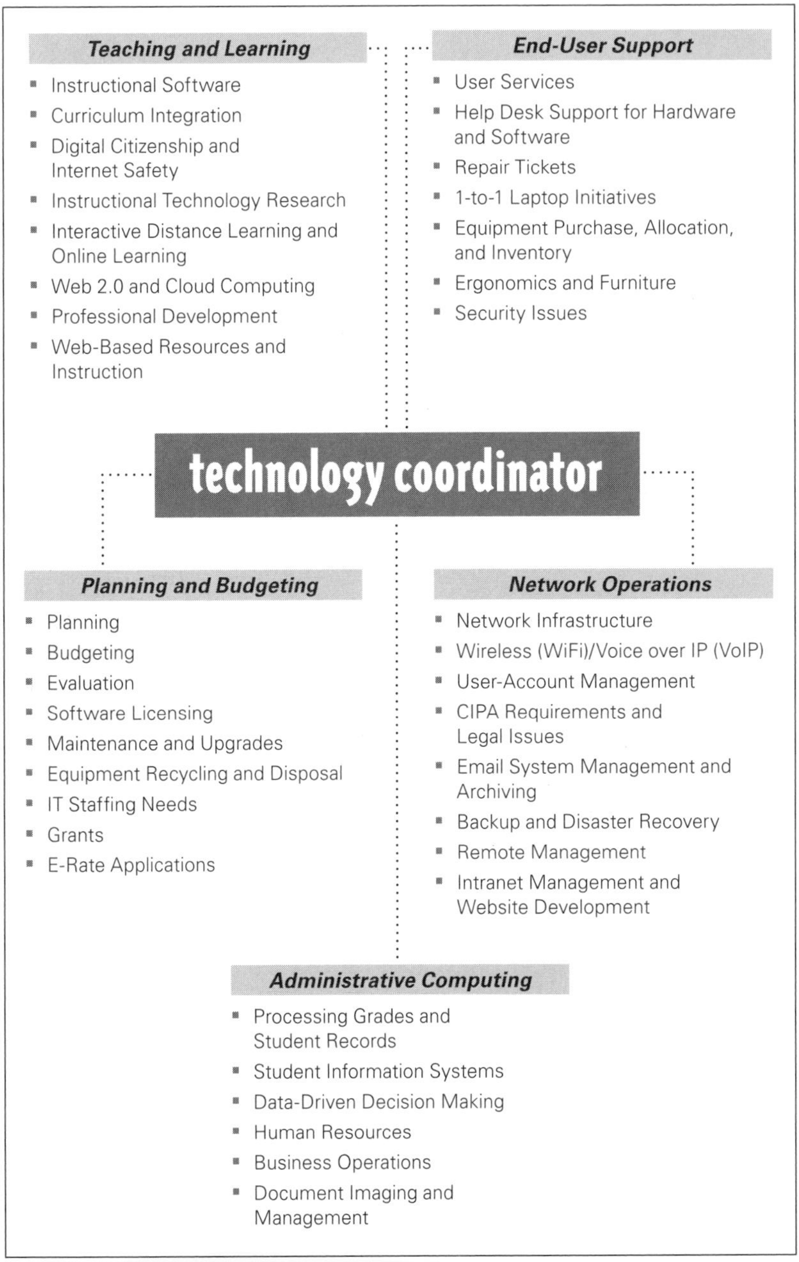

Teaching and Learning

- Instructional Software
- Curriculum Integration
- Digital Citizenship and Internet Safety
- Instructional Technology Research
- Interactive Distance Learning and Online Learning
- Web 2.0 and Cloud Computing
- Professional Development
- Web-Based Resources and Instruction

End-User Support

- User Services
- Help Desk Support for Hardware and Software
- Repair Tickets
- 1-to-1 Laptop Initiatives
- Equipment Purchase, Allocation, and Inventory
- Ergonomics and Furniture
- Security Issues

technology coordinator

Planning and Budgeting

- Planning
- Budgeting
- Evaluation
- Software Licensing
- Maintenance and Upgrades
- Equipment Recycling and Disposal
- IT Staffing Needs
- Grants
- E-Rate Applications

Network Operations

- Network Infrastructure
- Wireless (WiFi)/Voice over IP (VoIP)
- User-Account Management
- CIPA Requirements and Legal Issues
- Email System Management and Archiving
- Backup and Disaster Recovery
- Remote Management
- Intranet Management and Website Development

Administrative Computing

- Processing Grades and Student Records
- Student Information Systems
- Data-Driven Decision Making
- Human Resources
- Business Operations
- Document Imaging and Management

Figure 1.1 Technology Coordinator Issues Model (TCIM 2.0) overview

Real-Life Technology Coordinators

The following composite profiles depict the varying work environments and job descriptions typical of the technology coordinator position in small, medium, and large school districts around the country.

Meet Susan R.

Technology Coordinator for a Small Rural District

Susan R. works as the technology coordinator for a rural Midwest school district. She is the only technology staff member for the district, which serves an agricultural town of about 10,000 people. The district has five school buildings, with a total enrollment of 1,200 students in Grades K–12.

Susan serves the district as network administrator, performs hardware maintenance and repair, handles the purchasing and installation of equipment and software, manages the technology inventory, develops short- and long-range technology goals, and manages all technology spending. She provides professional development in technology for all employees of the school system. Her responsibilities also include directing the technology committee responsible for developing and carrying out the technology plan and for implementing technology integration activities in district classrooms.

Thanks to her considerable experience in working with schools and teachers, Susan has been successful in implementing special technology initiatives in her district. She was instrumental in initiating a plan providing middle school students with netbook computers—a program that has been successful with both teachers and students. One of the secrets to her success has been the development of a cadre of district teachers and administrators who assist her with planning, decision making, staff training, and implementation activities. Susan is also active in technology leadership activities in her state. She has twice served as the president of the statewide computers-in-education organization.

Susan came to this position from outside education and has never worked as a teacher. She received her computer training through a vocational program and does not have a four-year college degree. She has been working in this position for nine years and works on an 11-month-contract basis. Her salary range for this position is $35,000–$45,000.

Meet Sam T.
Technology Coordinator for a Medium-Sized Urban District

Sam T. is the general director of information services for a Midwest school district in a state capital with a population of 130,000. The district serves 14,000 students in Grades K–12, with 37 instructional sites and additional support sites, service centers, and office locations.

Sam deals with the management and administration of all aspects of information and communication technology for the district, including voice, video, and data services. His duties include development of the district technology plan, implementation of several technology-themed magnet schools, and planning and development of a high-speed network capable of carrying data, voice, and video to all schools. His office is responsible for budgeting, purchasing, installation, and support of all district technologies. His staff of 20 includes PC and network technicians, network administrators, help desk operators, professional development trainers, instructional specialists, programmers, computer operators, and technicians.

Sam began his work with information technology while serving in the Navy for 10 years. After leaving the military, he earned a bachelor's degree in education and worked as a secondary math teacher for several years. Later, Sam worked in the business field and gained experience in developing, implementing, and using information technology services in business.

Sam spent 12 years working for the district in various aspects of information technology before coming into his current position four years ago. He is earning additional college credit in educational administration coursework.

Sam and his technology team work on a 12-month-contract basis. The salary range for his position is $60,000–$70,000.

Meet Ted B.

Technology Coordinator for a Large Urban District

For three years, Ted B. has been the director of instructional technology for a diverse, urban school district in a Midwestern state's largest city. More than 100 instructional sites are located across this city of 400,000, serving more than 48,000 students in a wide variety of traditional schools, magnet schools, and special programs.

Ted has worked in education for 22 years as a classroom teacher, building administrator, and district administrator. He also worked at the state's department of education. Originally trained as an elementary teacher, he earned a master's degree in educational administration and has been working with different aspects of technology for the last eight years.

As a mid-level administrator for a large district, Ted supervises a staff of eight instructional technology specialists who promote and implement the instructional use of technology. They provide professional development in instructional programs; support special education projects using technology; and provide schools, teachers, and classrooms with support for using technology in a learning environment. Ted and his staff are also responsible for developing the district-level technology plan in collaboration with other departments and for writing grant applications for special projects that offer unique opportunities to use technology.

As part of a large urban district, Ted has the freedom to concentrate on the instructional aspects of technology. Other departments within the district handle hardware and software support, network services, purchasing and installation of computer equipment, and administrative computing functions, such as data processing.

Working in a large bureaucracy has both advantages and disadvantages. Ted and his staff are free to concentrate on strictly instructional issues, but often their work is dependent on the work of other departments. Developing positive relationships with these departments through frequent and effective communication has been essential.

Ted and his staff work on a 12-month-contract basis. The salary range for his position is $80,000–$90,000.

Essential Questions

1. What are the major responsibilities the technology coordinator will be expected to assume?

   The technology coordinator is expected to help establish the vision for technology in the school or district, create policies that support that vision, train staff to make progress toward the vision, and assist end users to solve problems associated with technology.

2. What skills and abilities will be needed to succeed in the position?

   To be successful in this position, the technology coordinator will need a combination of strong interpersonal skills, effective problem-solving skills, leadership and planning skills, and technical skills.

3. What day-to-day operational tasks will the technology coordinator most likely face?

   The technology coordinator will be expected to conduct professional development training sessions, work with users to solve problems and answer questions, communicate with vendors, meet with district administrators to plan or develop policy, and speak to community groups about district technology initiatives. The technology coordinator is often responsible for the management of other technology personnel, such as network administrators, computer technicians, help desk operators, and building-level technology specialists. The development and update of the district website and the administration of the district intranet are also regular duties that fall in the domain of the technology coordinator.

4. What qualifications and job requirements are typically expected of technology coordinators?

   As part of their position, technology coordinators are expected to provide leadership, build relationships, offer assistance, model effective usage, assist teachers and students, plan and evaluate hardware and software purchases, administer maintenance programs, and make budgetary decisions.

5. What type of leadership role will the technology coordinator play in the school or district?

The technology coordinator will be expected to assist the administration and the board of education in establishing the school or district technology plan. The coordinator is expected to ensure the success of all school or district technology initiatives—from budgeting to purchasing to training to troubleshooting—in order to make the district technology vision a reality.

Resources

Print Resources

Ausband, L. (2006). Instructional technology specialists and curriculum work. *Journal of Research on Technology in Education, 39*(1), 1–21.

Baylor, A. L., & Ritchie, D. (2002). What factors facilitate teacher skill, teacher morale, and perceived student learning in technology-using classrooms? *Computers and Education, 39*(4), 395–414.

Bushweller, K. (1996). How mighty is your wizard? *The American School Board Journal, 183*(5), a14–a16.

Durost, R. A. (1994). Integrating computer technology: Planning, training, and support. *NASSP Bulletin, 78*(1), 49–54.

Grohe, B., & Levinson, E. (2002). Managing technology is different. *Converge, 5*(1), 42–43.

Hoffman, B. (1996). Managing the information revolution: Planning the integration of school technology. *NASSP Bulletin, 80*(2), 89–98.

Holland, L., & Moore-Steward, T. (2000). A different divide: Preparing tech savvy leaders. *Leadership, 30*(1), 6–10.

Jewell, M. (1999). The art and craft of technology leadership. *Learning & Leading with Technology, 26*(4), 46–47.

Lesisko, L. (2005, March). *The K–12 technology coordinator.* Sarasota, FL: Paper presented at the annual meeting of the Eastern Educational Research Association March 2–5, 2005. (ERIC Document Reproduction Service No. ED490035)

Maddux, C. (2002). Information technology in education: The critical lack of principled leadership. *Educational Technology, 42*(3), 41–50.

Marcovitz, D. M. (1998). *Supporting technology in schools: The roles of computer coordinators.* Washington, DC: Society for Information Technology and Teacher Education Conference Proceedings. (ERIC Document Reproduction Service No. ED421150)

Moursund, D. (1992). *The technology coordinator.* Eugene, OR: International Society for Technology in Education (ISTE).

Ritchie, D. (1996). The administrative role in the integration of technology. *NASSP Bulletin, 80*(2), 42–51.

Online Resources

Re-defining the Role of the K–12 Technology Coordinator: http://aces.nmsu.edu/bchamberlin/techcoord/welcome.html

Technology Coordinator's Handbook home page: www.schools.pinellas.k12.fl.us/tchandbk/default.htm

Technology Coordinator Resources: http://exworthy.tripod.com/tc.htm

chapter 2

teaching
and learning

Essential Questions

1. How can the technology coordinator assist with the selection and purchase of effective instructional software?

2. How can the technology coordinator help teachers integrate technology into the curriculum?

3. What should the technology coordinator do to promote digital citizenship and assure Internet safety for students and teachers?

4. What instructional technology research should the technology coordinator do to investigate the effectiveness of technology use in classrooms?

5. How can the technology coordinator support the effective use of interactive distance learning and online learning?

6. What issues must the technology coordinator consider when implementing the use of Web 2.0 technologies and cloud computing?

7. How can the technology coordinator plan and implement an effective professional development program?

8. How can the technology coordinator use web-based resources to support teachers and students?

The work of the technology coordinator is important to all areas of the educational organization, but most crucially so in the areas of teaching and learning (Figure 2.1). It is in these two areas that technology coordinators can inspire teachers to use technology effectively in the classroom. In so doing, a technology coordinator can have a profound impact on student education and motivation.

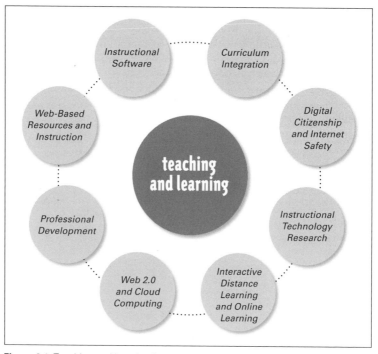

Figure 2.1 Teaching and learning issues

Selecting Instructional Software

The careful selection of instructional software is very important to the success of a school's or district's technology integration efforts. The technology coordinator must first determine which software will serve as the standard installation on each computer in the organization. This set of software comprises the basic set of tools available to all users.

Although districts may prefer one manufacturer over another, each computer should be outfitted with a minimum set of standard software: a word processing program for writing and editing text, a spreadsheet program for working with numbers, a database program for organizing and manipulating data, a page layout program for creating publications of various types, a presentation program for creating and organizing multimedia presentations, an email client for communicating, and a browser program to access the Internet.

This core software should become the basis for all machine setups and serve as the basic kit for the integration of technology into teaching and learning (McGillivray, 1999). Any users who access the technology resources within the organization can be sure they will find these standard tools installed and available for use. McGillivray points out that "because the tools are used across the curriculum, students learn to use them in multiple venues. Each teacher contributes to the student's mastery of the tools. By using the tools frequently, the student's mastery becomes more rapid and their work more sophisticated" (p. 46).

Figure 2.2 illustrates the software kit implemented by the Heidelberg Model Schools. This kit contains a set of common software programs that support the integration of technology into all classrooms and subject areas. By selecting common tools for communications, word processing, presentations, computation, reference, security, and administration, the school was able to minimize costs, provide universal access, and address a wide range of classroom activities and projects. The selection of common tools for all classrooms also minimized the support requirements because the number of programs was more manageable (McGillivray, 1999).

The programs included in the Heidelberg Model Schools software kit included some common resources installed on classroom computers in schools today. They are by no means the only choices a district can make in adopting a standard set of software tools for use by teachers, students, and staff. In addition to commercial programs such as these, a wide variety of freeware and shareware products are available from many developers and sources found on the Internet.

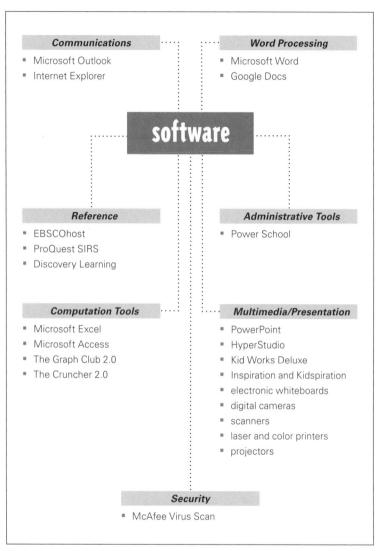

Figure 2.2 Software kit used by the Heidelberg Model Schools

Freeware and shareware products may lack the name recognition of more commonly known and used products, such as those shown in Figure 2.2, but they can offer similar functionality for a fraction of the cost. The OpenOffice suite of programs offers the same functionality as the more commonly known products from Microsoft and is essentially free to educational institutions. More information on this suite of programs can be found at www.openoffice.org. These programs are designed to share files and be interoperable with Microsoft programs.

Alternatives to Microsoft email services products also exist for both servers and classroom computers. Pegasus Mail offers the Mercury Mail Transport System for servers, as well as the Pegasus Mail client for individual computers. These are available as a free download from the Pegasus site (www.pmail.com). The software is free, but users do have to pay for user manuals and support. These fees, however, are minimal, even for a large organization. The Thunderbird email client, part of the Mozilla project, is another alternative to Microsoft products. Free downloads are available online (www.getthunderbird.com).

The technology coordinator also plays an integral role in the selection of additional software for use in the classroom. The coordinator must gather information about specific programs and vendors, locate and distribute software reviews, and compare the various programs' capabilities and determine how they might support the school's or district's goals for technology use and integration.

It is important that the tech coordinator solicit input from staff and teachers before making final software selections. These users will have a better understanding of the curriculum and how the software can support it, and they will ultimately be the ones to use the software to support learning. Allowing end users a strong voice in purchasing decisions will lead to greater support and, ultimately, more frequent use of the software. The coordinator can effectively guide this process by acting as the liaison who contacts vendors, conducts research on new programs, tests the software on district computers, contacts other schools or districts to see what products they are using, and reports to the school software committees that will make the final selections.

helpful hint

Online Database

It is important to make sure that software evaluation information is available to staff members searching for instructional software. Technology coordinators can create an online database of software evaluation information that can be easily accessed, viewed, and modified as products are reviewed. Publishing a database program, such as Filemaker Pro (www.filemaker.com), on a website makes it easy to share information over a network or the web. This program comes with 30 starter solutions that can be adapted to the user's particular needs. Creating and posting such a database will help staff members more easily find useful software and avoid wasting time with inferior products that someone else has already tried and reviewed.

The technology coordinator also plays a vital role in obtaining the best price for such purchases by engaging in the *bid request* process, working with consortia to make bulk purchases, and working with vendors to secure the best pricing available. Throughout the selection process, the technology coordinator should work to ensure that the software packages chosen match the educational goals and long-range technology plans for the school or district.

One way that technology coordinators can demonstrate their leadership and improve this process is to implement standard procedures for the selection of classroom software. Many valuable education dollars have been misspent on software programs that did not work as intended, were not compatible with or appropriate for the school's or district's hardware, or did not address an appropriate district educational need. An effective way to guard against this is to implement standard forms, criteria, and selection procedures for the purchase of instructional software.

The first step in this process should be to establish a software adoption committee. This committee—made up of representatives from different grade levels and subject areas—is charged with the evaluation of purchasing requests for instructional software programs. This committee should meet as needed to review software recommendations and work with the technology coordinator to make final purchasing decisions.

The technology coordinator should develop and use standard software selection

toolbox tip

Software Selection Form

Software selection is a time-consuming task that can benefit considerably from well-defined procedures. Making use of a software selection form can help standardize the process and make selection decisions more informed and effective. This form should identify useful information about the product and how it will be used in an educational setting. This information can be quite helpful when making software purchasing decisions.

forms to gather information about products that staff members wish to purchase. These forms should require staff members to gather basic product information, specify how the software would be used educationally as well as what content and technology standards it would address, list specific hardware requirements, and summarize relevant software review articles. The requestor should then be required to submit all of this information to the software selection committee. The software selection committee would then evaluate all requests, make selections based on the information contained in the requests, and work with the technology coordinator to make final purchasing and budget decisions.

software selection form

Name _____

School _____

Grade or Department _____

Software Title _____

Publisher _____

Content Area _____

Topic _____

Targeted Grade Level _____

TECHNICAL REQUIREMENTS

Computer/Processor Required		Hard-Drive Space Required	
RAM Required		Additional Hardware Required	
Compatibility with Existing Software		Other Requirements	

SOFTWARE CATEGORY

❏ Presentation

❏ Simulation

❏ Tutorial

❏ Reference

❏ Authoring

❏ Drill and Practice

❏ Other (please specify)

❏ Multimedia

❏ Data Processing

❏ Educational Game

❏ Graphics

❏ Handheld Application

❏ Word Processing

software selection form *(continued)*

TYPE OF LICENSE TO BE PURCHASED *(CHECK ONE)*

☐ Single Computer   ☐ Site License

☐ Lab Pack   ☐ Network License

SOFTWARE FEATURES

CLAIM	Strongly Agree	Agree	Disagree	N/A
The directions are clear and easy to follow.				
It is easy to start and exit the program.				
Users can easily resume where they left off in the program.				
The program functions well and is free of bugs.				
The program is enjoyable to use.				
The graphic elements are meaningful and appropriate.				
Sound can be turned on and off.				
The software contains useful management features.				
Basic tasks are easily learned and intuitive.				
Advanced features are easy to access and apply.				
Menu-driven tutorials are built into the program.				

software selection form (continued)

What specific curricular and technology standards will be addressed by this software?

_____

_____

What are your instructional goals for using this software?

_____

_____

Have you found reviews of this software? If so, summarize comments from the reviews:

_____

_____

Have you tested the software in the classroom? If so, summarize what you did with the software, and rate its usefulness to the learning process:

_____

_____

If you haven't used the software before, do you know colleagues who have? If so, indicate how they used the software and their general evaluation:

_____

_____

Other comments or information:

_____

_____

software selection form *(continued)*

PURCHASING INFORMATION

Cost _____

Product ID Number _____

Recommended Vendor _____

Vendor Address _____

Vendor Phone Number _____

Software Selection Committee Comments

_____

_____

Committee Purchase Recommendation   ☐ Yes   ☐ No

Technology Coordinator Notes

Date of purchase _____

Software license number _____

Installation information, notes, and location(s)

_____

_____

Tech Leader Profile 1

Jim Clark, Instructional Technology Specialist

Jim Clark is an instructional technology specialist for the Wichita Public Schools in Kansas. Wichita is an urban district located in the largest city in the state. Approximately 500,000 people live in this metropolitan area. The district serves more than 49,000 students and has a total of 97 schools, comprising 56 elementary schools, two K–8 attendance centers, 17 middle schools, 11 high schools, and a variety of other special schools and programs. Jim has worked in this position for the past 12 years. Previously, he served eight years as a high school science teacher at one of the Wichita high schools. He holds an MSE degree in science education as well as additional technology training certifications, including Microsoft Certified Systems Engineer, Cisco Certified Network Associate, and Palm Education Training Coordinator. The main responsibilities in his job are providing school-based professional development programs related to technology, providing district-wide technology-based workshops for teachers, and supporting district-level instructional technology initiatives. There are a total of ten people who work in the Instructional Technology Department for the Wichita schools, including a secretary and a program supervisor. Jim reports to the executive director of Instructional Technology for the district. His biggest challenges on a daily basis are in providing varying levels of leadership and support for district projects and initiatives that are, at times, in competition with other departments and priorities. Jim's tip for other technology leaders is to be patient and never forget that developing and maintaining relationships is a critical component for job success.

Integrating Technology into the Curriculum

The technology coordinator spends considerable time working with teachers to help them integrate technology into new or existing curriculum. It is easy for teachers to fall into the trap of assuming that the way they have been doing things for years is fully acceptable, even optimal. It is difficult, sometimes, to dissuade them from this notion and encourage them to try new things. As Wasser (1996) aptly points out, "Learning to function effectively in technologically rich environments is a complex developmental process for individuals and the systems in which they work" (p. 1). Changing the way teachers teach and use materials requires time, commitment, risk taking, adequate resources, and consistent and patient support. The technology coordinator needs to be able to inspire teachers with a vision of how effective technology integration can benefit them and then demonstrate activities, lesson plans, and processes that make exciting use of technology resources.

Technology coordinators can start this process by offering a variety of informal professional development opportunities from which teachers can learn more about the technology resources that are available for use in the classroom. By offering a variety of courses in an informal, collegial setting, the technology coordinator can familiarize teachers with new hardware and software resources without intimidating them. The coordinator can also listen to teachers' concerns and questions and clear up misconceptions.

Once teachers become comfortable using technology for their own purposes, they will find it easier to devise ways to implement the same technology in their classrooms. Technology coordinators can offer regularly scheduled technology sessions before or after school, during the lunch hour or planning time, or on a release-time basis. These sessions can be set up to teach a particular skill or introduce a new idea, but more important, they should establish a venue for teachers to experiment with technology and become comfortable using it. Study groups can be established, which provide an effective environment for teachers to study a new technology in depth and learn from one another as they develop their skills. Regardless of method, teacher training is critical to the successful integration of technology within the organization: "A one-size-fits-all professional development approach generally does not work in the face of the great diversity of technology readiness and ability" (Wasser, 1996, p. 3).

To ensure that teachers are provided with the training and resources they need, it is important for the tech coordinator to confirm that a standard set of technology resources is available in all classrooms,

toolbox tip

Mini-Grants

Mini-grants are a great opportunity to promote technology integration and provide incentive for staff to find new ways to use technology in their work. Offering larger grants for cooperative projects helps get more than one teacher involved. Teachers who have completed a mini-grant project should be required to offer a professional development session so that other staff members can learn from their experiences.

A mini-grant program could be funded in a variety of ways. Professional development funds from either the technology budget or the general professional development budget could be used to fund such a program. Grant funds from federal, state, or private sources could be used to support a mini-grant program if the grant were written to include the support. An example of a mini-grant application form can be found in Appendix B.

and that additional, specialized technology tools are available in libraries and media centers. A classroom should be outfitted with at least one multimedia classroom computer and such standard software as word processing, spreadsheet, database, and desktop publishing programs, as well as an email client and Internet browser. Libraries or computer labs should be furnished with additional equipment such as digital cameras, scanners, image-editing software, storage devices, *CD* and *DVD* burners, and digital video editing equipment. Providing a variety of resources in various locations around the school helps ensure that teachers and students have ready access to the resources they need to carry out myriad learning activities.

To enhance the use of technology in classrooms, it is often beneficial for a technology coordinator to organize and administer a mini-grant program that provides special funding for new and innovative projects. Mini-grant programs can provide seed money for special projects that emphasize technology integration at the classroom level. They can fund the purchase of special hardware and software, additional training for teachers, release time for teacher preparation and planning, or travel to conferences to learn new techniques and ideas. This kind of program can put new technology resources directly into the hands of students and have a dramatic impact on teachers' attitudes toward technology integration.

Digital Citizenship and Internet Safety

Digital citizenship is a theme that is part of the ISTE standards for students, teachers, and administrators. An organization that adopts this theme is, in effect, formally recognizing that educational technology users must be prepared to accept the cultural, legal, and ethical responsibility of appropriate use of digital information and resources. Mike Ribble, author of *Digital Citizenship in Schools, 2nd Edition* (2011), describes digital citizenship as "a concept which helps teachers, technology leaders, and parents to understand what students and other technology users should know to use technology appropriately." Often, students (and adults) misuse technology because it is unclear to them how technology resources should be used in an appropriate way. Helping students, teachers, and others to understand how to appropriately operate in a new and sometimes confusing environment is one of the challenges the technology coordinator must be prepared to face.

Since the passage of the Children's Internet Protection Act (CIPA) in 2001, schools taking part in the *E-Rate* program have been required to have an Internet safety policy in place. This policy requires schools to implement Internet filtering capabilities to protect students from obscene, pornographic, or other harmful material. The passage of the Protecting Children in the 21st Century Act in October 2008 has resulted in several changes to the CIPA requirements. These changes affect a district's Internet safety policy. Students must now be educated about appropriate online behavior, such as when using a *social network* and other online communication services (for example, chat rooms). These new requirements also mandate that Internet safety policies make certain that students receive education regarding *cyberbullying*. Beginning on July 1, 2012, school boards must update their current Internet acceptable use policy or create a new policy that requires Internet safety be taught.

These issues fall under the broader theme of digital citizenship, and helping both teachers and students understand digital citizenship issues is an important task for the technology coordinator. If a district is serious about implementing technology standards (such as those developed by ISTE), the inclusion of digital citizenship standards will be a natural part of the instruction. It is important that such instruction takes place in district classrooms so that the requirements of CIPA are met and the Internet safety policy is implemented.

Addressing the issue of digital citizenship and safe Internet behavior is an appropriate and prudent role for schools to adopt. Many students (and teachers) have moved beyond the simple use of technology in their classrooms and homes, and have begun to take part in larger digital communities through the use of social networking tools and applications. It is important for them to understand how to use these resources in a safe and ethical way. And it is important for the technology coordinator to assist teachers and students in understanding the appropriate types of information that should be shared over the Internet, steps that should be taken to keep private information private, and understanding the standards for behavior and interaction when using technology resources both at school and at home.

Just as inappropriate behavior happens when groups of adolescents gather face to face, inappropriate behavior can occur when adolescents use technology. Today's technology offers a level of anonymity that may cause youthful technology users to write messages or post comments that they would never say in person. Online bullying behavior, called cyberbullying, must be anticipated, monitored, and dealt with in a timely fashion. Schools must work with students to help them understand appropriate behavior and encourage proper use of technology resources at school and home. In addition, educators must help both students and parents understand the hazards of online bullying behavior. The technology coordinator must work to make sure the appropriate policies and procedures are in place, that teachers and other school officials understand appropriate online behavior and instruct students about the school's policies, and have developed plans for how to deal with instances of misbehavior and bullying. Just as educators must be prepared to deal with bullying behavior on the playground, so, too, they must be prepared to deal with cyberbullying behavior in the library or classroom.

Conducting Research on the Effective Use of Technology

The technology coordinator is frequently expected to conduct research and gather data pertaining to the effectiveness of *instructional technology* use in the school or district. While the data may be solely anecdotal, such data can still be valuable in analyzing how teachers and students use technology resources, as well as determining how that use can be optimized. This information may be shared with the board of education, presented to the community at large, or showcased through local media outlets.

Technology coordinators can gather useful information by using both standard surveys and online tools such as the following:

- The ProfilerPro online assessment tool from Advanced Learning Technologies in Education Consortia (ALTEC), http://profilerpro.com

- The Levels of Teaching Innovation (LoTi) Framework developed by Chris Moersch, http://loticonnection.com

Both of these online tools assist teachers and educational leaders in assessing their knowledge, skills, and ability to effectively use technology in education.

Once this type of information has been gathered and analyzed, it can be used by the technology coordinator, administration, technology planning committee, and even curriculum planning committees, to analyze the impact technology is making across the curriculum. This data can help the technology coordinator understand what is currently happening with technology in the school or district, how this use fits with current curricular standards, and what progress is being made toward reaching the goals set forth in the school or district technology plan. The results can be used to make necessary modifications in the

toolbox tip

Standardized Surveys

Using standardized surveys to gather information from staff members can be an effective way of obtaining data on the use of technology in the classroom. These surveys can also help determine the need for additional professional development for staff.

Unfortunately, it is often difficult to get survey respondents to complete and return materials in a timely manner. As well, the amount of returned materials can be insufficient, which then makes the survey an ineffective measure. If getting survey results from all staff members is important to the question or questions being studied, then the technology coordinator can organize a formal gathering. Such a gathering can be a faculty or staff meeting, team time, or a special meeting. Regardless, the technology coordinator must explain the purpose of the survey, detail reasons for its importance, and provide time for respondents to complete the materials.

Completing surveys in these types of settings also allows the technology coordinator to answer questions from staff. Taking the time to complete a survey in this way ensures full participation and provides meaningful data for analysis.

curriculum and determine if current standards are being met.

The technology coordinator who wishes to conduct systematic research and evaluation of technology in a school or district would benefit from examining two publications of the U.S. Department of Education. *An Educator's Guide to Evaluating the Use of Technology in Schools and Classrooms* was published in 1998 to evaluate the Technology Literacy Challenge Fund (Quinones, Kirshstein, & Loy). This guide is intended to assist superintendents, technology coordinators, principals, professional development directors, teachers, and parents who have little or no experience conducting research. While the guide was developed some time ago for a program that is no longer in existence, it remains a useful resource for understanding how to proceed in developing a manageable evaluation process.

This guide offers a variety of helpful suggestions and ideas, including a flowchart of the evaluation process, examples of formative and summative evaluation questions, tips on where to begin, data that should be collected, questions to ask, and forms and worksheets to use in the process. The guide also contains a variety of sample surveys that can be used as is or can be adapted to meet the particular needs of a given evaluation project.

Technology in Schools: Suggestions, Tools and Guidelines for Assessing Technology in Elementary and Secondary Education is a publication developed by the Technology in Schools Task Force and funded by the National Center for Educational Statistics (Ogle, et al., 2002). This publication was developed to help decision makers prepare, collect, and assess information about if and how technology is used in their school systems. It is organized by seven primary topics and important key questions. These topics include technology planning and policies, finance, equipment and infrastructure, technology applications (software and systems), maintenance and support, professional development, and technology integration. For each of these topics, key questions are identified and guidance is given on how best those questions can be answered through the collection of data and records.

Although this document is quite useful in identifying both the questions and the information necessary to answer the questions, ultimately it is up to those conducting the evaluation to determine if their needs and goals are being met.

Interactive Distance and Online Learning

Schools have been delivering distance education programs of various types for more than half a century. One of the earliest of these programs involved students in the outback areas of Australia. These students learned via the Alice Springs School of the Air, which began radio broadcasts to students on remote ranches beginning in 1951 (Hannay & Newvine, 2006). Lessons have been taped and lectures broadcast to students in many locations. They have even been beamed by satellite to students on military bases or assigned to naval vessels. A number of schools have established distance education classrooms that allow students in multiple locations to see and interact with one another through specialized classroom equipment, including cameras, microphones, projectors, and document cameras to display materials. These specialized classrooms have helped to transform distance learning from early radio transmission of lectures into *interactive distance learning* experiences in which students see, hear, and interact with both the teacher and students regardless of geographical location.

Improvements in Internet-based resources and web technologies, coupled with the increased availability and falling cost of broadband connections in homes, has made videoconferencing, web meetings, online video, and advanced content delivery systems part of the online learning experience. Online distance learning in K–12 schools has often taken the form of "virtual schools or cyber schools operated by entities that may include school districts, charter schools, consortia, for-profit companies, and nonprofit organizations" (Rice, 2006).

Schools have implemented distance education and online learning programs for a variety of reasons. Distance education classrooms that can link to multiple locations have been established in schools to share the services of a teacher among schools or even among districts from a single location. This allows schools to share the cost of a specialized teacher, such as a foreign language or advanced math instructor. Online programs have been implemented to establish cyber schools or virtual schools. These virtual schools provide access for students who cannot attend regular classes for health or other reasons and, in some cases, attract students from other locations who become official students of the host district by taking part in the online program. These programs can also be popular among nontraditional students who may desire a program that can be completed on their own schedule and without the structure required when attending a traditional school.

Schools offering virtual programs often promote the benefits of these educational experiences. These benefits may include increased motivation, expanded access, increased student choice, and administrative efficiency (Cavanaugh, Barbour, & Clark, 2009). Although there may be certain advantages to students enrolled in these virtual programs, there are also a variety of challenges for an organization offering such programs. These challenges include high startup costs, accreditation of online schools, retention of students, and providing all necessary services and support necessary for the program to be successful.

The technology coordinator may be faced with a variety of challenges in providing the equipment, resources, and support necessary to assist the school organization with establishing and maintaining either a distance learning or virtual learning program. An expensive variety of equipment and telecommunication services are necessary for such programs, and it is important that the technology coordinator work effectively with vendors and service providers to establish the necessary resources. Teaching strategies and techniques that are effective in a traditional classroom may not easily transfer to the distance education or online programs. For distance and online learning to succeed, teachers need support and professional development in establishing and implementing materials, resources, activities, assessments, and other best practices. In addition, teachers need ongoing technical support and assistance for working with the specialized instructional delivery systems of an interactive distance classroom. Robust and reliable connections, messaging systems, chat rooms, discussion boards, online video presentations, and web meeting systems are all components of a successful program. The technology coordinator must be prepared to help teachers step outside their comfort zone, take risks, explore new tools and resources, and learn new ways of providing a caring and effective learning environment for students.

Web 2.0 and Cloud Computing

The tools, capabilities, and resources available on the Internet have grown and matured. We have entered the era of *Web 2.0.* The term Web 2.0 usually refers to Internet-based applications and capabilities that allow people to connect to one another and share information. Web 2.0 activities include writing a *blog,* sharing ideas through Twitter, connecting with people via a social network like Facebook, or using Internet-based applications like Diigo or Google Docs. Although the term Web 2.0 often means various things to different people, its capabilities have several implications for the technology coordinator.

Because Web 2.0 applications and tools connect people through *social media* tools and social networks, sharing information and making connections with others are the focuses of many Web 2.0 users. Hardman and Carpenter (2007) point out that "the social networking features of today's Internet can be useful tools for connecting staff, students, and parents." Creating and sharing classroom and school information through blogs and *wikis,* demonstrating student learning by developing and posting student *podcasts* or videos, or creating personal learning networks for teachers via Twitter, Delicious, or Skype are some examples of Web 2.0 educational activities. Using Web 2.0 tools to partake in social networking activities may lead to increased student engagement, provide an authentic audience for students, and allow new ways for teachers and students to create, collaborate, and participate in learning activities that require critical thinking and deeper levels of learning. As Klein (2008) states, "it is possible to create a safe, comfortable, relevant environment for students, teachers, and staff to create, collaborate, and grow in."

Teachers and staff members will likely need training and assistance in implementing new web-based technologies in the classroom. Although students may already be using some of these technologies at home, teachers may need training and support in order to embrace the idea of blogging, creating wiki sites, sharing resources through Delicious, or developing students' podcasts or video productions. The technology coordinator may also need to think ahead and craft policies and procedures that address the new capabilities available with Web 2.0 technologies. Technology coordinators can begin to address the use of Web 2.0 and social networking tools by updating the district acceptable use policies or student codes of conduct. These guiding documents were often developed with classroom computers and *local area networks* in mind and may not address the capabilities, issues, or potential risks that connecting with others through the Internet may pose.

Web 2.0 applications and services are capable of providing functionality once reserved for local computers or networks. This idea, called *cloud computing*, has created a significant buzz in the technology community. As well, there is considerable interest among users to have their computing applications and services delivered through Internet connections. The anytime and anywhere capability of cloud computing offers a variety of potential advantages and challenges for the technology coordinator to consider when making decisions about what (if any) of these capabilities to implement in a district.

Cloud computing services have many different names and are offered by a variety of vendors. Users of these services may (Google tools, for example, are free) pay a fee for the use of storage or application capabilities. In turn, the client organization does not incur the actual cost of providing the capability. Instead of needing copies of an application and servers to run the application, a district simply pays for a subscription for use. This allows users of the service (online storage, web page or wiki development tools, or other applications) to access their files and information from any computer with an Internet connection. The use of cloud computing makes it possible for users to think of computing as an anytime or anywhere capability. Files and tools can be accessed from school, home, or anywhere one can connect to the Internet. This allows convenient and easy access to information and work projects, and makes sharing and collaborating possible.

Although cloud computing capabilities offer a variety of conveniences and benefits to an organization, the decision to subscribe to such services should not be made without careful consideration of a number of issues. While the use of cloud computing services frees a district from the cost of equipment purchase and maintenance, the cost of the necessary account subscriptions should be compared and considered carefully. Before moving to cloud-based services, a district must also make sure that the necessary network connectivity capabilities are in place. A recent conversation with a technology coordinator shows why. The coordinator had made the decision to move to Google Apps for Education rather than use a local computer-based application. After implementing this change, a variety of network problems began to pop up. Testing of the local network connections showed usage levels of more than 130%, which slowed network traffic to a crawl. The technology coordinator was forced to make significant investments in network equipment and expand network connection capacity in order to meet the new cloud-based computing requirements.

The technology coordinator must carry out sufficient analysis, evaluation, and planning in order to effectively implement cloud computing and serve end users. In addition, policies and procedures may need to be updated to reflect changes brought about by cloud computing capabilities. Users must be provided with the necessary guidelines for using these updated district computing resources.

Planning and Implementing a Professional Development Program

One of the most challenging and important tasks a technology coordinator will face is the creation of a professional development program for all employees of a school or district. Effective professional development was one of the four pillars for technology use in schools that was described in 1996 by President Bill Clinton. He articulated this vision through the Technology Literacy Challenge Fund. The four pillars of this initiative are:

1. Provide all teachers the training and support they need to help students learn through computers and the information superhighway.

2. Develop effective and engaging software and online learning resources as an integral part of the school curriculum.

3. Provide access to modern computers for all teachers and students.

4. Connect every school and classroom in America to the information superhighway.

A successful professional development program allows a school district to prepare teachers (and, in turn, students) to use technology as a natural part of the curriculum.

Often a district begins by teaching "tool"-related courses to teachers and staff. These courses help people more effectively use their computers and installed software programs. These types of courses do not do much, however, to help teachers learn how to integrate technology into their instructional practices. Effective professional development programs focus on the larger goal of improved student learning and performance, rather than on learning technology as a goal in and of itself: "Learning to use Microsoft Word is not the same process as learning to teach writing across the curriculum using Word" (Peterman, McGillivray, & Frantz, 1998, Hanau American Schools section, para. 13).

The technology coordinator must work with teachers and the school or district administration to determine professional development needs and design a program to meet those needs. A good place to begin is with a review of the district or building technology plan. The technology plan is the guiding document that lays out the road map of where the organization wants to go with technology and how it plans to get there. To develop an effective technology professional development program, the program must be tied to the goals and intentions of the larger plan for technology in the district. Reviewing the district technology plan helps the technology coordinator and other stakeholders clearly understand what sorts of skills and dispositions are important and what work needs to be done to design a program that will develop them.

When planning a technology professional development program, it is important for leaders to look at the national standards for students, teachers, and administrators. The International Society for Technology in Education developed these standards in conjunction with a variety of educational leadership organizations, curriculum organizations, the U.S. Department of Education, and several private organizations. More information about these standards, along with a variety of supporting resources, can be found at www.iste.org/standards. These standards provide guidance on what skills should be learned, when they should be taught, and how technology can be used to support new learning environments. They have been adopted by most U.S. states and serve as the basis for the standards used in many other states, private schools, and in countries around the world. These standards and related resources provide a solid basis for determining what teachers and administrators should learn as part of a technology professional development program.

No professional development program will be successful unless it acknowledges the skills people already have and what they already know. It is important for a technology coordinator to have an understanding of the thoughts and desires of the people who take part in a professional development program. By conducting a series of focus group conversations with teachers and staff members who represent various departments, grade levels, and schools from across the district, it will be possible for the tech coordinator to have a clear understanding of the staff's professional development needs.

Surveys and other assessments are useful tools for investigating the technology needs and skill levels of district staff. A variety of online tools and resources exist for conducting such surveys and assessments. Chris Moersch has developed a helpful assessment tool with his Levels of Technology Integration (LoTi) surveys, which can be found online at www.loticonnection.com. Another useful tool for self-assessment of staff technology skills is the ProfilerPro online collaboration tool from Advanced Learning Technologies in Education Consortia (ALTEC), found online at www.profilerpro.com. This free tool allows users to take surveys online to assess their technology skills and abilities. The site also includes access to surveys based on the ISTE standards. Technology coordinators can also use these online tools to develop and modify surveys of their own and then download data results.

Once the technology coordinator has gathered all the pertinent information from focus group conversations, surveys, and other assessments, an effective program can be planned and implemented. The program should include a variety of learning opportunities and interventions that are available in a number of different formats. Teachers may learn by taking classes, working individually with the technology coordinator to develop and teach lessons, participating in a study group, attending a conference, collaborating with other staff members on a technology project, or all of the above. Without this training and support, teachers are likely to use the technology resources available to them only for lower-level tasks, such as word processing. Those who have received the necessary assistance and training, on the other hand, tend to use technology for higher-level activities such as data collection and analysis, complex problem solving, and Internet research. Effective professional development supports teachers' efforts to integrate technology broadly and deeply into their professional practice and school life (Wasser & McNamara, 1998).

While the technology coordinator often focuses most on the teaching staff and their use of technology to enhance learning, it is important not to overlook other groups when planning professional development programs. Staff members from various departments, office staff, and administrators all have a need for appropriate professional development. From learning to use computers for record keeping to effectively managing and analyzing information to learning the newest administrative computing software package, the technology coordinator should consider how to provide the necessary professional development for these groups as well.

Finally, consideration should be given for providing professional development and training opportunities for the technology staff, including the technology coordinator. These individuals are often overlooked when considering professional development needs, yet they work in a rapidly evolving and changing field. Providing opportunities for learning and growth to the technology staff will lead to increased knowledge, skills, and better support for all technology users in the district.

Tech Leader Profile 2

Heather Hurley, Instructional Technology Coordinator

Heather Hurley is the instructional technology coordinator for Arlington Traditional Elementary School in Virginia. Arlington is an urban school district that is part of the Washington, D.C. metropolitan area. This district is made up of 36 different schools including 22 elementary, five middle, and three high schools that serve nearly 19,000 students who come from 127 different nations and speak 105 different languages. Arlington Traditional Elementary School serves 425 students and has 36 faculty positions. Heather has worked in this position for three years and has spent a total of 16 years in education.

Originally trained as an elementary and special education teacher, Heather has earned an MEd in instructional technology and is currently working on a graduate certificate in school administration aligned with the NETS•A standards for school administrators. She also has earned designations as a SMART Master Trainer and is a STAR Discovery Educator. The technology department for Arlington Public Schools is divided into two divisions: Information Services, which includes technicians, information systems, and network services; and Instructional Technology Services, which concentrates on instructional technology.

Heather is one of 34 instructional technology coordinators working across the Arlington district, and she reports directly to her school principal. Her main responsibilities are technology integration, professional development/training, and technical support. Heather's biggest challenge is making sure the school staff views her as a curriculum specialist, rather than simply someone responsible for fixing computers and hooking up equipment. Her tip for other technology leaders is "Create an expectation that technology is an instructional tool that requires goals and benchmarks for success. Also, make sure that school administration clearly understands what technology integration is and how a technology coordinator supports this type of integration."

Incorporating Web-Based Resources and Instruction

The Internet offers the technology coordinator marvelous resources for use in the coordinator's own job position, and it is also a wonderful source for instructional materials: "The Internet, more so than any technology that has preceded it, provides students with access to a vast array of information and resources far greater than could ever be provided within the four walls of a classroom" (U.S. Department of Education, 2000a, p. 31). The tech coordinator should be adept at finding and organizing the wide array of resources and materials that exist on the Internet in order to inform classroom teachers about them.

The technology coordinator should also find ways to share and publicize some of the many sites and resources that can enhance instruction. A technology coordinator can create a links section for the district website. This site can be updated regularly and can contain organized and categorized links to resources on the Internet. Another method for sharing information of this type is through a regular publication, either print or electronic, that lists resources for classroom use. Such an in-house newsletter can be used to showcase resources and draw attention to sites that teachers may want to visit and use in their teaching.

Working with teachers to integrate technology into the classroom is often the most rewarding aspect of a technology coordinator's job, and it certainly offers the greatest potential for directly affecting student learning and performance. Creating professional development opportunities, from which teachers can learn new techniques and try them out in a safe and supportive environment, can lead to significant changes in classroom practices.

Successful technology integration is a time-consuming and recursive process that requires a great deal of encouragement and support. Teachers will go through various comfort-level stages as they learn about and use technology. The fundamental changes in teaching practices that technology often requires do not happen overnight. This three- to five-year process requires risk taking and commitment from staff, ongoing professional development, and a long-term commitment to offering appropriate technical and instructional support.

ANSWERS TO
Essential Questions

1. How can the technology coordinator assist with the selection and purchase of effective instructional software?

    The technology coordinator can enhance the selection of software by introducing the use of standard software tools (sometimes referred to as a toolbox approach); establishing a software selection committee; implementing such management practices as using forms for making selections; and setting up standardized procedures to be used throughout the selection process.

2. How can the technology coordinator help teachers integrate technology into the curriculum?

The technology coordinator must make sure that teachers have a variety of opportunities to learn about the use of technology in the classroom. They must also have access to the resources they need to successfully integrate technology into their teaching practices. Offering mini-grants or other incentives will encourage teachers to invest the time needed to incorporate technology into their teaching in meaningful ways.

3. What should the technology coordinator do to promote digital citizenship and ensure Internet safety for students and teachers?

The technology coordinator must work to make sure the appropriate policies and procedures are in place, and that teachers and other school officials understand appropriate online behavior. The tech coordinator must instruct students about the school's policies and have developed plans for how to deal with instances of misbehavior and bullying.

4. What instructional technology research should the technology coordinator do to investigate the effectiveness of technology use in classrooms?

By making use of anecdotal research and encouraging teachers and school leaders to use the online research and planning tools available from ALTEC, the LoTi Framework, and other resources, the technology coordinator can assure that data are being gathered about the use of technology in the school or district. Student assessment data can also be a useful source of information. This data should be used to evaluate current educational programs and make modifications as necessary.

5. How can the technology coordinator support the effective use of interactive distance learning and online learning?

The technology coordinator must be prepared to work with the specialized delivery systems of interactive distance classroom connections and online learning environments in order to provide the technical support and assistance those users of the service need. It is important for the technology coordinator to assist teachers in moving outside their comfort zone, taking risks, exploring new tools and resources, and discovering new ways to provide a caring and effective learning environment for students.

6. What issues must the technology coordinator consider when implementing the use of Web 2.0 technologies and cloud computing?

   The technology coordinator must sufficiently analyze, evaluate, and plan in order to effectively implement both Web 2.0 capabilities and cloud computing resources. The technology coordinator must also ensure that policies and procedures are updated so that users are provided with the necessary guidelines for effectively using district computing resources.

7. How can the technology coordinator plan and implement an effective professional development program?

   The technology coordinator creates an effective professional development program by working with staff and administration to determine the needs of the staff, designing learning opportunities to meet those needs, and implementing a program of opportunities that will assist teachers in linking the use of technology to the learning goals and objectives of the school or district.

8. How can the technology coordinator use web-based resources to support teachers and students?

   Web resources can be shared with staff and students by posting them to a links section of the district's website or by sharing them through a regular publication that highlights resources of interest to teachers and students.

Resources

Print Resources

Bull, G., & Ferster, B. (2006) Ubiquitous computing in a web 2.0 world. *Learning & Leading with Technology, 33*(4), 9–11.

Cavanaugh, C., Barbour, M., & Clark, T. (2009). Research and practice in K–12 online learning: A review of open access literature. *International Review of Research in Open and Distance Learning, 10*(1). (ERIC Document Reproduction Service No. EJ831713)

Hardman, J., & Carpenter, D. (2007). Breathing fire into web 2.0. *Learning & Leading with Technology, 34*(5), 18–21.

Klein, J. (2008). Social networking for the K–12 set. *Learning & Leading with Technology, 35*(5), 12–16.

McGillivray, K. (1999). The tool kit: An innovative approach to technology integration in networked schools. *Learning & Leading with Technology, 26*(5), 45–49.

Ribble, M. (2011) *Digital citizenship in schools* (2nd ed.). Eugene, OR: International Society for Technology in Education (ISTE).

Rice, K. L. (2006). A comprehensive look at distance education in the K–12 context. *Journal of Research on Technology in Education, 38*(4), 425–448.

Wasser, J. (1996) Navigating schools past the technology on-ramp. *Hands-On! 19*(2), 14–16.

Wasser, J., & McNamara, E. (1998). *Professional development and full school technology integration.* Hanau Model Schools Partnership Research Brief #5. Cambridge, MA: TERC.

Online Resources

CEO Forum on Education and Technology. (1997). School technology and readiness report: From pillars to progress. Available from www.eric.ed.gov/ERICWebPortal/recordDetail?accno=ED416819

CEO Forum School Technology and Readiness Chart: www.eric.ed.gov/ERICWebPortal/detail?accno=ED437382

Hannay, M., & Newvine, T. (2006). Perceptions of distance learning: A comparison of online and traditional learning. *MERLOT Journal of Online Learning and Teaching, 2*(1). Available from http://jolt.merlot.org/documents/MS05011.pdf

The Innovative Educator's Tech Assessments page: http://theinnovativeeducator.wikispaces.com/Li's+Tech+Assessments

International Society for Technology in Education (ISTE): www.iste.org

ISTE National Educational Technology Standards Project. Available from www.iste.org/standards

Learning Forward (formerly the National Staff Development Council): www.learningforward.org

Levels of Technology Integration (LoTi) Survey: www.loticonnection.com

Mid-continent Research for Education and Learning (McREL) Technology Resources: www.mcrel.org/topics/EducationalTechnology

National Center for Education Statistics (NCES), National Forum on Education Statistics, and U.S. Department of Education, Office of Educational Research and Improvement (2002). *Technology in schools: Suggestions,tools, and guidelines for assessing technology in elementary and secondary education*. Washington D.C.: U.S. Department of Education. Available from http://nces.ed.gov/pubsearch/pubsinfo.asp?pubid=2003313

ProfilerPro. Online Collaboration and Assessment Tool: www.profilerpro.com

Quinones, S., Kirshstein, R., Loy, N. (1998). *An educator's guide to evaluating the use of technology in schools and classrooms* (Report No. ORAD-1999-1200). Washington, DC; Office of Educational Research and Improvement. Available from www.eric.ed.gov/ERICWebPortal/recordDetail?accno=ED425740

U.S. Department of Education. (2000). *e-Learning: Putting a world-class education at the fingertips of all children*. Available from: www2.ed.gov/about/offices/list/os/technology/reports/e-learning.pdf

chapter 3

end-user
support

Essential Questions

1. What types of services must the technology coordinator be prepared to provide to technology users in the organization?

2. How can the technology coordinator optimize help desk support for end users?

3. What must be done by the technology coordinator to ensure that repair tickets and support requests are attended to in a timely manner?

4. What must the technology coordinator know about 1-to-1 laptop initiatives in order to provide the support necessary to make such an initiative successful?

5. How can the technology coordinator ensure that the purchasing, allocation, and inventory of equipment is carried out in an effective manner?

6. What must the technology coordinator know about ergonomics and the selection of furniture for offices and classrooms?

7. How can the technology coordinator effectively protect computers from viruses, worms, and other security threats?

The technology coordinator's primary role is to support the end users of technology throughout an organization. The technology coordinator must be prepared to provide support services to many different types of end users, including students, library clerks, classroom teachers and school administrators. Figure 3.1 identifies some of the important support services that technology coordinators provide to end users.

Figure 3.1 End-user support issues

User Services

In any school organization there are many different types of users. Each user type needs technology for a wide variety of purposes, from office projects to scientific investigations to digital art projects. These many types of users require many different sorts of assistance as they make use of technology in different ways and for different purposes.

It is the challenge of the technology coordinator to effectively support all of these user types. The support services range from equipment selection, purchase, installation, initial training, classroom integration, repairs, and replacement. In order for the technology coordinator to offer high quality support to district technology users, he or she must provide more than troubleshooting or repair services.

Students and administrators rely on technology to complete assignments or job duties. Teachers rely on technology to provide an effective learning environment for their students. A technology coordinator must understand the unique needs of each user type, and then provide a wide range of support services in a timely and effective manner. In so doing the technology coordinator becomes, in effect, a customer service manager.

This ideal is not easily achieved. A survey by the National Center for Educational Statistics on school technology use for fall 2008 (Gray, Thomas, & Lewis, 2010) revealed that 31% of public schools reported having a full time staff member responsible only for technology support and integration. This survey also indicated that half of public school users often wait up to eight hours for assistance with software problems or questions, and wait from two to five days for equipment repairs. End-user support is a challenge for technology coordinators in schools across the nation. The specific requirements for support are diverse, and the demand for services will continue to grow as the use of technology expands in schools.

The technology coordinator is often caught between the demands of the teaching staff (whose focus is supporting students and meeting student achievement standards) and the desires of the IT staff (whose focus is on maintaining an optimal infrastructure). The technology coordinator must be able to bridge the gap between these two groups. As a technology support leader, it is important that the technology coordinator listen to all sides of an issue and then find a solution that meets the needs of all groups and end users.

Help Desk Support for Hardware and Software

Teachers and staff members frequently need on-site and on-demand technical assistance, both with equipment and software and with the implementation of the technology in the classroom. Standard and effective procedures must be in place for providing timely assistance to users and for solving software and hardware problems. Nearly two-thirds of all teachers polled in 2000 reported that the lack of technical support or advice was a barrier to their use of technology (U.S. Department of Education National Center for Education Statistics, 2000).

One established method that has been used successfully in many industries is a dedicated *help desk*. A help desk is a technical assistance center, contacted by phone or email, that provides users with immediate help for technology-related questions or problems. When users encounter a problem, they place a call to a help desk operator who, in turn, has considerable experience with the hardware and software used by the organization. The help desk operator will assist the user by answering questions, explaining procedures, or diagnosing problems. The operator first attempts to guide the user in solving the problem on his or her own. Help desk operators might be members of the technology staff, or they may be members of a student technology support group, which have become increasingly common in schools across the nation.

If the creation of a help desk is not possible, it is still important for a technology coordinator to establish consistent and responsive support procedures. By establishing procedures for requesting assistance and communicating them throughout the organization, technology coordinators can let teachers and staff members know what technical help is available and how to access it.

Small districts that lack the funds to create an actual help desk staff position may rely on a help desk email address. Users can send questions and requests for assistance to this address, which is managed by the technology coordinator. A number of schools across the country have successfully recruited teachers to serve as technology support contacts (Murray, 2001). Teachers who provide technical support and training may be given a reduced teaching load or receive extra compensation in exchange for their help.

As mentioned previously, students can also be a valuable resource in this regard. The Generation Yes program, started in 1996, prepares students to solve problems and assist teachers with the use of technology in the classroom. Students in the program pair up with a partner teacher. The teacher provides expertise with software and hardware, and then the student and teacher collaborate on the creation of learning projects that use technology, such as a help desk. The Generation Yes program has been successfully implemented in many schools across the nation, and in 2000 it was recognized by the U.S. Department of Education as an exemplary program. More information about this program can be found at www.genyes.org/freeresources.

The Cisco Networking Academy is another technical-training program available to students. Launched in October 1997, the Networking Academy is now available in all 50 states. Academies are located in high schools, technical schools, colleges, universities, and community-based organizations. The academies provide technical training that leads to Cisco certification in networking skills. More information about these academies can be found at the Cisco Networking Academy website: www.cisco.com/web/learning/netacad.

Technical assistance may also be available through an organization called Tech Corps. Using a Peace Corps–like model, Tech Corps works to recruit volunteers to assist schools with technology. Tech Corps has created several programs that link teachers and students with IT professionals who then provide advice and guidance. These IT professionals come from a variety of backgrounds and can provide assistance with various technology issues, and even offer career information to students with an interest in technology. To learn more about this program or to enroll as a participant, visit the Tech Corps website at http://techcorps.org.

Tech Leader Profile 3

Geoff Miller, Director of Technology

Geoff Miller is director of technology/alumni coordinator for the American Overseas School of Rome. He has worked at the school since 1997, has held his current position since 2001, and is a 1967 graduate of the school. The American Overseas School of Rome, a single, private school located in Rome, Italy, currently has an enrollment of 630 students and a staff of 120, including faculty and administration. He supervises a hardware technician (the only other person in the technology department) as part of his responsibilities.

Geoff reports directly to the head of school. A graduate of UCLA with a degree in ancient history and archeology, Geoff completed a master's degree in instructional technology from Duquesne University in December 2009. He is also certified by Microsoft for both networking and operating systems. Geoff has spent 25 years of his career as the owner and manager of one of the largest music stores in central California, acquiring a background in sales, marketing, sound system installations, and recording studio technology. He is also certified by many musical instrument manufacturers, including Gibson and Martin (the worldwide leading companies in guitar construction), to repair and restore their instruments. He spent three years teaching elementary school computer classes and three years teaching computer graphics at the high school level. In his current job, Geoff's three main areas of job responsibilities are network maintenance and management, technical support and professional development for faculty and administration, and website management and marketing development. The biggest daily challenge Geoff faces is the development of new strategies to promote and continue the integration of technology into the curriculum.

Working at a private school in Europe, U.S. federal and state mandated competencies do not apply. The ongoing implementation and improvement of instructional technology is his single most important focus for enhancing student learning in the 21st century. Geoff's tip for technology leaders is to get everyone involved in the "business" of technology as early as possible. Because users often feel that technology tends to be an externally implemented phenomenon, an effective technology leader helps these users understand that instructional technology is neither "external" nor a "phenomenon." If technology does not already permeate all aspects of students' lives, both personally and professionally, it will in the future. Thought of in this way, educators can use technology as a strategic tool in the classroom.

Repair Tickets

Although the help desk is an important first line of support for end users, the time will come when a problem cannot be solved by telephone or email. On-site technical assistance will be needed. When a classroom computer breaks down, it is important to return its functionality to the user as soon as possible so that work can be continued (McClure, Smith, & Sitko, 1997).

The technology coordinator must create a *repair ticket* system to initiate on-site technical assistance and document the necessary repairs to a particular piece of equipment. Such a system can operate in a variety of ways. We are aware of one district that asks users to send an email request to a special email address (e.g., workorders@ourschool.org). A technology staff member monitors this email account and either replies with repair information, such that users can solve the problem themselves, or places the request on a schedule for a visit by a technician.

Other districts have created a paper document that is filled out and sent to the appropriate contact person at the building or district level. One such district uses a multipart form: one copy goes to the technician, one goes to the scheduling secretary, and the third is kept as a record of services provided. Still other districts have users file requests for service online through a special page on the school's or district's website. This type of electronic reporting allows for a considerable amount of information to be gathered regarding problems and solutions. Such a system also allows technicians to use any Internet-connected computer to check on reported problems and requests for service, thus reducing the time necessary to resolve the problem.

Whatever method of reporting problems that a school or district uses, once a problem has been documented, the support staff can prioritize the problem and create a plan for initiating the necessary repairs or service. Simple problems—when the equipment is still operational, but the user is experiencing difficulties—may be given a lower priority. Higher priority problems—if a piece of equipment is totally inoperable, for example—the support staff may decide to attempt repairs immediately.

Priority may also be assigned by establishing a hierarchy of locations. One method for making such a determination is to evaluate the number of students or staff members affected by a given problem. For example, support for school offices might be priority number one, followed by libraries, computer labs, and then individual users.

By using standard procedures to collect, document, and plan responses to technical problems and equipment failures, it is possible to ensure that problems are resolved in a timely manner. This documentation is also useful in determining the effectiveness of the technology-support operation. Work orders and support-request documentation can allow the technology staff to monitor when problems have been solved, how they were solved, and which still need attention. This documentation also provides a record of the diagnosed causes of recurring problems, the amount of service required by individuals and buildings, and other trends in the technical services being provided. A database that tracks problem computers, problem programs, and problem users can make a world of difference in the efficiency of a technical-support operation.

Information gathered from a documentation system can be used proactively as well. By examining the time necessary to close out a work order, the technology coordinator can monitor the efficiency of the department. Such information can also be used in determining if the department has the necessary technical personnel to provide the level of service desired. Such reports on technology services can provide useful data for administrators or board of education leaders. These statistics and data can also be used to provide background during budgeting discussions, which is especially important when advocating for additional funding or personnel designed to improve the services available to district users. Users may also be asked to complete a survey to determine satisfaction levels with the current service. These surveys can allow for user feedback, which helps technology coordinators improve departmental operations and customer satisfaction.

1-to-1 Laptop Initiatives

Many schools across the nation have implemented *1-to-1 laptop initiatives*, which essentially means that one laptop computer is provided to each teacher and student. The intent is to increase the use of technology in the classroom, maximize student engagement, and ultimately raise test scores (the aim of virtually all educational innovations of recent years). The 1-to-1 laptop movement is based on work that began in the 1980s with the Apple Classrooms of Tomorrow (ACOT) project, which was the first to bring 1-to-1 computer access to schools. Maine was the first state to implement a large-scale student laptop project. Launched in the fall of 2002, the Maine Learning and Technology Initiative provided laptops to all seventh and eighth grade students and their teachers. Another large project, started in the fall of 2004, was the Technology Immersion Project (TIP) conducted by the Texas Education Agency. In this program, laptops were provided to teachers and students at 22 different middle schools.

Based on the initial findings of these research projects, and anecdotal evidence suggesting that such innovations improve student achievement and provide other educational benefits, more and more schools are endeavoring to implement 1-to-1 laptop initiatives in their schools. While such a project may seem as simple as providing computers to students, the success of a 1-to-1 initiative requires a variety of end-user support services.

The purchase of laptop computers and placement of these computers with students in classrooms is only the first, and perhaps the easiest, step in a long and complicated process. A survey of 74 Indiana school administrators (Clausen, Britten, & Ring, 2008) noted that just because laptops were available and in use did not necessarily mean that technology was becoming integral to instruction. These administrators observed that often the use of technology was at a low level, such as word processing or searching for information. Weston and Bain (2010) point out that often "what does exist are replacements: books replaced by web pages, paper report cards with *student information systems,* chalkboards with interactive whiteboards, and filing cabinets with electronic databases." While all these initiatives begin with the best of intentions and the promise of significant progress, lack of a clear vision and the need for a shift in the educational paradigm are necessary for ongoing success.

Rolling out a successful 1-to-1 laptop initiative requires significant planning, investment, training, and ongoing support. Providing the laptops is a step that must follow significant planning by a committee of involved stakeholders who are able to develop a detailed and well-considered plan for the project. Several programs have provided laptops to teachers first, well in advance of student implementation, for advanced training and curricular planning. Proper implementation of technology requires that technology coordinators provide effective technical support for the equipment and network systems. In addition, technology coordinators must ensure that teachers are provided with professional development opportunities, especially in the areas of technology skill assistance and instructional planning. Infrastructure planning and decisions must be made for electrical, network, and wireless capabilities. Policy and procedure decisions must be made to establish clear expectations for appropriate use and care. Significant initial resources, as well as ongoing funds for support and training, are necessary to ensure the success of such projects.

Equipment Purchasing, Allocation, and Inventory

Part of using technology successfully is selecting the most appropriate equipment for a given situation. Equipment that does not meet the needs of the end user can lead to user frustration. These users will simply stop using the equipment. Technology coordinators are usually responsible for planning and purchasing the technology that will be used throughout the school or district. In order to make appropriate purchases and assignments, the technology coordinator must have a solid understanding of how equipment will be used. A computer that is appropriate for a fourth-grade classroom may not be appropriate for a computer-assisted drawing lab or an administrative office. Learning how to allocate the school's or district's technology resources most effectively and equitably is a crucial aspect of the technology coordinator's support role.

The technology coordinator should work with end users to develop the specifications for equipment to be purchased. It is helpful to have different sets of specifications for each setting: one set of specifications for a standard classroom computer, for example; one for a specialized computer lab; one for an office computer; and so forth. A setting will determine software and hardware needs: the amount of memory required, how much access to network resources is necessary, the size of monitors that will be suitable, and the proper number of inputs for plugging in peripherals. Each computer may be based on a particular model from a manufacturer, but the technology coordinator should determine different options depending on the needs of the user and the distinctive way in which the machine will be used.

After general specifications have been developed in consultation with end users, the technology coordinator should obtain current pricing from a variety of retailers or manufacturers. Prices should then be compared. This price comparison is usually done through a competitive bid process.

A formal bid request describes the specifications of the item to be purchased, provides a timeline for when the bid must be returned, and sets a time and date for a formal bid opening. It is essential to accurately spell out all requirements in the bid request, including machine features, requirements for parts, length of warranty, and technical support issues. Failure to address an issue may lead to problems and frustrations after the purchase is complete.

The following pages show a form that requests sealed bids for the purchase of 15 projectors.

request for bid

UNIFIED SCHOOL DISTRICT

123 Elm Street

Anywhere, OR 97409

Date   May 24, 20xx

Bid No.   0304-C-10

To   Jane Smith

Sealed bids addressed to USD Purchasing Department will be received at (mailing address) until 2:00 p.m. PST on June 15, 20xx, at which time the bids will be opened and read aloud. Bid envelope shall be plainly marked:

> **SEALED BID FOR PROJECTORS**
>
> **DO NOT OPEN BEFORE**
>
> **DATE: JUNE 15, 20xx, 2:00 P.M. PST**

Any bid received later than the specified time, whether delivered in person or mailed, shall be disqualified. The district reserves the right to reject any or all bids, to accept the bid deemed most advantageous to the school district, and to waive any formalities of bidding.

All bidders whose domicile is located outside the state should furnish the school district with a copy of their state's preferential bidding statutes and the applicable percent received by in-state bidders from the state in which the contractor is located.

John Brown

(Purchasing/Property Manager)

School District #383

request for bid (continued)

BID NO. 0304-C-10 Projectors

DUE: June 15, 20xx, 2:00 p.m. PST

BID SPECIFICATIONS

This bid is for 15 projectors with the following specifications.

Technical specifications for computer projectors

Screen brightness	*Minimum 2,000 ANSI lumens*
Contrast ratio	*400:1*
Projection lamp	*200 watt UHP*
Lens type	*Manual zoom and focus*
Estimated lamp life	*2,000 hours*
Throw distance	*4 ft. to 25 ft.*
Native resolution	*1024 x 768 (XGA)*
Display compatibility	*SXGA, XGA, SVGA, VGA*
Computer formats	*1280 x 1024, 1024 x 768, 800 x 600, 640 x 480*
Computer inputs	*Two required: one DVI and one component in/monitor out*
Video inputs	*RCA and S-Video*
Cable	*DVI to VGA cable included*
Remote projector & mouse control	*Wireless (infrared) with laser pointer*
Carrying case	*Carrying case must be included*
Weight	*7 lbs. or less*
Warranty	*Three-year/6,000-hour projector warranty*

request for bid (continued)

BID NO. 0304-C-10 Projectors

DUE: June 15, 20xx, 2:00 p.m. PST

We have read all guidelines stated in the notice to bidders and submit this quotation in accordance with stated conditions.

Authorized Signature _____

Date _____

Company Representing _____

Questions concerning this quotation may be directed to

_____

(please print or type name)

Telephone Number _____

Fax Number _____

Email _____

Approximate delivery date _____

Bid prices good through _____

Price per projector _____

Quantity x 15 _____

Total Bid Price _____

The recent economic recession has created a variety of challenges for school technology budgets. With large numbers of people out of work, tax collections have dwindled, which has caused state and federal support for schools to decrease significantly. Providing an adequate technology budget and funding for technology support staff has been one of many economic challenges for school districts. Many districts have endured several years of declining technology budgets, and schools may face several more years of limited or decreasing technology funds. It likely will be an ongoing struggle for districts to find the resources necessary to purchase needed equipment replacements, upgrade existing technology, and provide adequate levels of essential support services.

For those school districts looking for ways to reduce hardware costs or maximize the purchasing power of their budgets, a few ideas for getting the most from hardware dollars are listed below:

- Consider factory-refurbished equipment. This equipment includes items that have been used for demonstrations, are cosmetically damaged, and have been designated as factory-defective systems. All are repaired and tested by the original equipment manufacturer (OEM). These items have been recertified to meet the original equipment specifications and are often sold with a warranty. The purchase of such equipment can yield considerable savings.

- Consider equipment that is coming "off-lease" with another organization. This is the equivalent of purchasing a program, or fleet, car from a used-car dealer. The equipment would be from one to three years old when returned from the lease. All equipment is cleaned, repaired, and certified to meet original standards. While neither new nor the latest model, such equipment may meet the needs and requirements of the district for general purpose use. As with a program car purchase, the district would save significant amounts through the purchase of such equipment.

■ Consider the purchase of used equipment that has been refurbished by a commercial reseller rather than an OEM. Such equipment is available from a variety of commercial resellers across the country.

■ Consider a purchase of surplus equipment from a large organization or a government entity. Surplus equipment is not necessarily defective or obsolete but is equipment that has been removed from service because it is no longer needed or has been replaced by newer equipment. Many government entities have programs for dealing with surplus items. An example of one such program is found in Missouri. The state requires that all surplus technology equipment be transferred to its surplus property program and made available to all public entities in the state. You can find more information about this program online at www.oa.mo.gov/purch/surplus.html. Such programs exist for most states, as well as the federal government. A web search should provide the contact information you need to access such a program in your own state.

Once the selection, purchase, allocation, and installation of equipment have been completed, the technology coordinator must see that an accurate technology inventory is established and maintained. An asset inventory provides critical information regarding what technology resources exist and how they are allocated. Inventory data are important to the technology planning process, budget planning, and decision making,

---

toolbox tip

Drive Image

When ordering a large number of pieces of equipment, it may be useful to contract with the vendor to preinstall the desired *drive image* prior to shipment. With volume purchasing it is often possible to have a machine shipped to the school or district for software installation and setup. This machine's setup then becomes the "master" image, which the manufacturer can duplicate for all subsequent computers prior to shipping. If *cloning* machines prior to shipping is not possible, loading drive images on a local server or an external hard drive and then cloning on site may be an acceptable alternative.

and provide the district organization information about long-term return on investment.

Management of the technology inventory can be challenging for organizations of any size and may prove especially complex for large organizations. A variety of software solutions are available to help technology coordinators and other IT professionals manage this complex and often frustrating task. Zenworks from Novell (www. novell.com/products/zenworks) offers the technology coordinator the ability to gather asset inventory information through the district network. Other solutions, such as Track-It! from Numara (www. numarasoftware.com), provide the tracking of technology assets through the network, in addition to providing work-order management capabilities.

How the technology coordinator chooses to manage the district inventory—manually, through an existing asset control system, or through one of the products mentioned here—is a matter of choice by the district. The critical issue is that the district technology inventory is established and kept up-to-date. This will prove important for technology planning, budgeting, E-Rate applications, and the conveyance of information to district decision makers regarding the technology resources available in the district.

Tech Leader Profile 4

Kevin J. Galbraith Sr., Executive Director of Technology

Kevin Galbraith is the executive director of technology for the Wayne-Westland Community Schools in Michigan. Wayne-Westland, a suburban district 20 miles west of downtown Detroit, serves seven communities and is among the 15 largest districts in Michigan with nearly 13,500 students. The district is made up of 26 schools, including 17 elementary schools, four middle schools, two traditional high schools, a technical high school, an alternative high school, and an early childhood facility.

Kevin has served as the technology director for the past six years and in similar positions for a total of 11 years. He reports to the deputy superintendent for Educational Services in this position. Originally trained as an elementary teacher, Kevin holds an MA in educational psychology with a concentration on technology as an instructional tool and has earned additional graduate hours in supervision and administration. He has also received training in IT project management and has earned a school technology management certificate from Michigan School Business Officials. The state of Michigan has no official licensure or certification for technology leadership positions. Kevin supervises a technology department of 12 people who, along with three repair technicians, are responsible for a fiber-optic network connecting 5,300 computers, 2,500 telephones, 1,200 printers, and a wide variety of related technology equipment, in addition to the district's student information system.

His main responsibilities are (1) to maintain the district technology plan in support of the district mission and vision; (2) to set the goals to achieve the plan, including budget development, purchasing, and managing timelines; and (3) to be the central communicator about the technology plan—building consensus about the plan and ensuring that the organization is moving forward with the plan. Kevin identifies effective communication as his greatest challenge in being an effective technology leader. To be successful in his position, he must communicate with students, teachers, administration, parents, and the community at large. Kevin's tip for other technology leaders is, "Don't forget to make time to participate in your own professional learning community. It is so easy to get lost in the day-to-day problems of budgets, metrics, and repairs that we lose focus on teaching and learning. If it's not happening in the life of a student, we should be carefully looking at why ... or why not."

Ergonomics and Furniture Selection

When considering the purchase and installation of equipment, the technology coordinator must think carefully about *ergonomics* and about how regular technology use will affect the health of users. Computer equipment should never be set up on desks or tables that are intended for another purpose or activity. Desktop, chair, monitor, and keyboard heights should be carefully coordinated to minimize neck and eye strain and avoid hand and wrist injuries. The positioning of the mouse, the lighting, and the overall working environment should also be evaluated when setting up work areas.

Because portable devices such as laptops, handheld devices, and tablets are by definition easily moved from area to area, it is critical that users learn the correct way to use these devices ergonomically. This attention to ergonomic details will help students and staff to avoid both discomfort and the repetitive-motion problems associated with the use of technology.

Monitors and screens should be installed at a viewing height comfortable for the user. The top of the monitor should be aligned with the user's eyes and should be 15 inches to 25 inches away from the user's head when sitting normally. It is important to minimize glare. If a classroom, lab, or office has windows, position viewing devices so that they do not face them. Desks that have recessed monitors can be used in locations where the desks will be used for multiple purposes in addition to computing. The use of LCD or flat screen monitors help reduce the users' exposure to radiation that comes from a normal cathode ray tube (CRT) monitor.

If students will be using adjustable chairs designed for adults, it may be helpful to lower the armrests, raise the seat, and push the lumbar support forward. If chairs do not have these adjustments, you can place a pillow on the seat and behind the lower back. If feet dangle in this position, support them by providing some type of suitable footrest. Sitting perfectly upright is not recommended; users should relax and keep slightly open angles, while receiving proper support.

If students frequently work from papers or a textbook, consider providing document holders. These allow books and papers to be placed closer to the monitor and at a more ergonomic angle. Positioning them close to the screen minimizes the need for users to turn and twist their heads while working.

It is also important that workstations have adjustable keyboard trays to accommodate users of various sizes. Arms should lie close to the body, not outstretched or reaching to the side; elbows should be at a 90-degree angle, or greater; and wrists should be neutral (i.e., at about the same level as forearms).

Attention to such details will help students learn good work posture and avoid many of the problems associated with long-term office work.

Security Issues

All technology coordinators must be concerned with protecting computers from *viruses* and other threats to security. Because most computers are now connected to the Internet, infection from viruses, *worms*, and *Trojan horses*, as well as other damage to security, can cause considerable harm. The tech coordinator is usually responsible for implementing plans and procedures for protecting a school's or district's technology resources.

The first line of defense in computer security is the installation of virus detection software on all computers. Because new viruses are being created and discovered almost daily, this software must be updated on a regular basis. In addition, virus definitions must be kept current to provide the maximum protection available. Most virus software can be configured to automatically update the virus definitions on a weekly basis. The technology coordinator and other technical staff are responsible for making sure appropriate protection software is installed, correctly configured, and updated regularly.

Network servers also need protection from viruses. Servers usually require special versions of antivirus programs that are designed to provide protection in a server environment. For instance, Symantec offers Enterprise and Corporate, special editions of their antivirus products that protect servers. When purchasing antivirus software, it is important to purchase the additional licensing needed to acquire these specialized products that provide server-based security and protection. Failure to do so may allow a single user to infect all files stored on the server.

Additional products can be purchased that allow the scanning of email messages for infected attachments. Although implementing such products can protect users from viruses that are spread through the broadcasting of email messages containing infected files, it is also important to train users to follow basic rules of safe computing, which help to avoid virus infection and other security threats. Network managers can mitigate these risks by setting up the email server to filter out specific types of attachments (such as .exe and .cmd files), but users still must be trained to follow procedures such as saving and scanning attached files and programs before opening to avoid spreading viruses throughout the organization.

Managers must also be sure that network operations are safe from intrusion by outsiders. Firewall devices and programs should be used to protect the network from outsiders who try to gain access and steal valuable information. A firewall can be a program running on one of the network servers or a device installed as part of the network. Firewalls scan network traffic and block unknown outsiders from using network resources. They also serve to protect the servers and clients attached to the network from hackers and malicious invasion programs designed to cause problems. Just as school staff protects school property from invasion and robbery by locking doors, implementing a firewall on a network protects hardware, software, and clients from invasion by intruders or programs such as viruses or worms.

Another important security procedure is the backing up of critical data to removable media or a network resource. Training users to take the time to carry out a regular *backup* procedure protects them from a variety of problems related to virus infection or machine failure. If regular backups of data are made, even if a virus infects a machine or the machine is compromised in some other way, critical information and work will not be lost.

Although not technically viruses, *spyware* and *adware* are becoming considerable problems for IT departments in schools and businesses. These two types of programs collect information about the user, pop up annoying advertisements on the screen, steal *passwords,* and waste both network and workstation resources. These programs may be installed on a user's computer during a visit to a questionable website or through the installation of another program without the user's knowledge. Once installed, they can cause a variety of computer problems, in addition to the gathering of user information.

Ad-Aware and Spybot Search and Destroy are two excellent programs that can identify and remove this type of software on a PC. Ad-Aware from Lavasoft is a free program for removing adware and can be downloaded at www.lavasoft.com. Spybot Search and Destroy, a free program for identifying and removing a wide variety of spyware programs, can be downloaded from www.safer-networking.org. For Mac users, Sophos offers free malware protection that can be downloaded at www.sophos.com.

Passwords can also be a security problem for those who manage computer networks. Users often choose passwords that are easy to remember but are also easy to crack by those who wish to gain illicit access to a computer network. Requiring users to change passwords on a regular basis helps avoid these problems. Educating users about good password procedures—such as choosing passwords that combine words, numbers, and symbols—will help keep networks more secure. Users should also be trained to never leave unattended computers logged onto the network; network managers can enforce this to some extent by setting the server to log off users whose workstations have been idle for a set amount of time.

To summarize: If a good antivirus software is in place and the software is always current, a basic level of protection will be achieved for all school or district hardware. Users who are trained to follow good security procedures will help keep virus infections to a minimum. Users must learn to avoid opening email messages from unknown senders and should scan unexpected attachments for viruses before opening or saving. It is also important for users to be cautious of clicking links in email messages without knowing where the link leads. Such links may connect to sites that can infect a computer or install unwanted programs. In addition, users must learn to exercise care when browsing unfamiliar sites. Simply visiting an unfamiliar site may initiate the installation of malware programs. It is important to educate users to be smart about sites they visit and what links they choose to follow. When users learn to consistently make backups of critical data and follow virus avoidance procedures, even a serious virus outbreak will not cause significant problems for users. Requiring users to change passwords, and teaching proper procedures for secure password creation and appropriate network use, will help avoid unauthorized network access.

ANSWERS TO
Essential Questions

1. What types of services must the technology coordinator be prepared to provide to technology users in the organization?

   The technology coordinator must be prepared to provide a wide variety of services to district technology users. These services may include consultation, equipment selection, purchasing, installation, training, troubleshooting, repair services, or curriculum integration. While the technology coordinator may not personally provide these services, preparations must be made for providing these services in a timely manner to district users.

2. How can the technology coordinator optimize help desk support for end users?

   Procedures must be created for providing technical assistance and support for users with questions or problems. Providing a central contact point for technology assistance and support will provide timely assistance to users and increase user comfort and satisfaction when using district technology resources.

3. What must be done by the technology coordinator to ensure that repair tickets and support requests are attended to in a timely manner?

   Establishing an appropriate system for documenting repair tickets and support requests is an important part of the end-user support that must be provided by the technology coordinator. Effective procedures must be in place to allow users to document the need for support or repairs and for tracking the resolution of those support requests. Providing a system for effectively documenting and responding to these support needs will allow the technology coordinator to offer effective user support services to district users.

4. What must the technology coordinator know about 1-to-1 laptop initiatives in order to provide the support necessary to make such an initiative successful?

   The technology coordinator must be prepared to help stakeholders establish a clear vision for the project; provide assistance with equipment, training, policies and procedures; and provide ongoing support in order to make a 1-to-1 project a successful investment of time and resources for the district.

5. How can the technology coordinator ensure that the purchasing, allocation, and inventory of equipment is carried out in an effective manner?

The technology coordinator should work with end users to develop the specifications for equipment to be purchased. School districts looking for ways to reduce hardware costs or maximize the purchasing power of their budgets should consider various purchasing strategies and sources. The technology coordinator should review the technology plan and consult with district and building leaders when making allocation decisions. A variety of software solutions are available to help technology coordinators manage the technology inventory and keep this critical information up to date.

6. What must the technology coordinator know about ergonomics and the selection of furniture for offices and classrooms?

The proper setup of technology equipment can have health benefits for users. Providing appropriate furniture and creating a comfortable work environment will help users avoid problems such as headaches and eyestrain.

7. How can the technology coordinator effectively protect computers from viruses, worms, and other security threats?

The technology coordinator must implement a multifaceted strategy for protecting technology resources. Network equipment and workstations must be protected from virus threats through the installation and regular update of antivirus software. Users must be trained in proper procedures for avoiding problems with virus infection. It is also important to implement procedures to help district users avoid problems with spyware and adware. These procedures should include information and training about how to avoid the installation of these types of programs, as well as how to use tools that will allow for the easy removal of these programs.

Resources

Print Resources

Anderson, A. (2009). Can't we all just get along? *Learning & Leading with Technology, 37*(4), 21–23.

Bateman, B. (2001). Maximizing your hardware investment. *Technology and Learning, 22*(3), 10–12.

Bateman, B. (2002). Installation made simple. *Technology and Learning, 22*(8), 46–48.

Breiner, B. (2009). Creating tech wizards. *Learning & Leading with Technology, 36*(7), 24–27.

Carter, K. (2000). Staffing up for technology support. *Technology and Learning, 20*(8), 26–33.

Clausen, M., Britten, J., & Ring, G. (2008). Envisioning effective laptop initiatives. *Learning & Leading with Technology, 36*(2), 19–22.

Donovan, L., Hartley, K., & Strudler, N. (2007). Teacher concerns during initial implementation of a one-to-one laptop initiative at the middle school level. *Journal of Research in Technology and Education, 39*(3), 263–286.

Durost, R. A. (1994). Integrating computer technology: Planning, training, and support. *NASSP Bulletin, 78*(1), 49–54.

Foa, L., Schwab, R., & Johnson, M. (1996). Upgrading school technology. *Education Week, 15*(32), 40–52.

Gray, L., Thomas, N., & Lewis, L. (2010). *Educational technology in U.S. public schools: Fall 2008* (NCES 2010-034). U.S. Department of Education, National Center for Education Statistics. Washington, DC: U.S. Government Printing Office. Available from http://nces.ed.gov/pubsearch/pubsinfo.asp?pubid=2010034

Johnson, L., Smith, R., Levine, A., & Haywood, K., (2010). *The 2010 Horizon Report: K–12 Edition*. Austin, TX: The New Media Consortium. Available from http://wp.nmc.org/horizon-k12-2010

Marcovitz, D. M. (1998). *Supporting technology in schools: The roles of computer coordinators*. Washington, DC: Society for Information Technology and Teacher Education Conference Proceedings. (ERIC Document Reproduction Service No. ED421150)

McClure, P. A., Smith, J. W., & Sitko, T. D. (1997). *The crisis in information technology support: Has our current model reached its limit?* Boulder, CO: Association for Managing and Using Information Resources in Higher Education CAUSE Paper Series No. 16. (ERIC Document Reproduction Service No. ED403837)

Murray, B. (2001). Tech support: More for less. *Technology and Learning, 22*(4), 40–44.

Owens, A. (2009). Do your teachers need a personal trainer? *Learning & Leading with Technology, 36*(8), 14–17.

Weston, M., & Bain, A. (2010). The end of techno-critique: the naked truth about 1:1 laptop initiatives and educational change. *The Journal of Technology, Learning, and Assessment, 9*(6). Available from http://escholarship.bc.edu/jtla/vol9/6

Online Resources

Association for the Advancement of Computing in Education (AACE): www.aace.org

AVG Technologies (an inexpensive antivirus alternative to McAfee or Norton): www.avg.com

Consortium for School Networking (CoSN): www.cosn.org

Frisk Software International's F-PROT (an inexpensive antivirus alternative to McAfee or Norton): www.f-prot.com

Insight Technology Solutions: www.insight.com

International Society for Technology in Education (ISTE):
www.iste.org

Lavasoft's Ad-Aware: www.lavasoft.com

Microsoft Volume Licensing: www.microsoft.com/licensing

Novell Worldwide Volume Licensing and Buying Programs:
www.novell.com/licensing

Numara Software's Track-It!: www.numarasoftware.com/track-it

Sophos Antivirus for Mac Home Edition: www.sophos.com

Spybot Search & Destroy: www.safer-networking.org

Tech Corps: http://techcorps.org

U.S. Department of Education, Office of Educational Technology:
www2.ed.gov/about/offices/list/os/technology

chapter 4

network operations

Essential Questions

1. How can the technology coordinator ensure that the network infrastructure meets users' needs?

2. What issues will confront the technology coordinator when providing Wireless (WiFi)/Voice over IP (VoIP) services to district users?

3. How can the technology coordinator assist with the management of network user accounts?

4. What role should the technology coordinator play in helping the district to meet the legal requirements of the Children's Internet Protection Act (CIPA)?

5. How can the technology coordinator assist with the management of the district email system, including archiving?

6. How can the technology coordinator ensure that appropriate backup and disaster recovery procedures are regularly carried out?

7. How can the technology coordinator use remote management tools to provide better network service and support?

8. What role should the technology coordinator play in the development and management of the district intranet and public website?

The computer network is the central nervous system of a school building or district. This network ties together the many different offices, classrooms, and other locations so that a school can use technology effectively and provide quality educational services to students. A school network supports efficient email communications, convenient access to database files, security for private documents and information, and access to shared resources such as printers and network-based programs. A computer network also makes it possible to take advantage of the information and resources that can be found on the Internet.

A computer network has a variety of benefits for the technology coordinator. The network makes it possible to monitor and manage resources, as well as to monitor usage by staff and students. The technology coordinator can use the network to create a shared storage area for staff members that remains invisible to student users. A network can make regular backups of both critical data and personal files. In addition, the network can be used to monitor the various devices and resources that are attached to the network.

A computer network also has a variety of advantages for staff and student users. A common storage area can be created so that staff or students can share documents and other information. Teachers can create a class folder on a shared network drive in which all students can save their work in individual folders. The files stored there can be made available to students in any location with network access: the computer lab, classroom, or library. As well, these files can be automatically backed up on a regular basis. The network makes it possible for users to work from many locations to access, share, and manage information.

The Internet has quickly become an indispensable resource for schools. It provides a wealth of information, and allows students and teachers to learn in new and different ways. Access to a computer network and the resources of the Internet allows users to connect to information sources in their local area, in other states, or on the other side of the globe: "When students communicate with people in distant and foreign places they begin to understand, appreciate, and respect cultural, political, environmental, geographic, and linguistic similarities and differences" (Rogers, 1996).

The Web-Based Education Commission called on legislators to "embrace an 'e-learning' agenda as a centerpiece of our nation's federal education policy" (U.S. Department of Education, 2000a). The federal government has also identified Internet access as a critical component of providing technology literacy for students. The first of five goals in the 2000 National Technology Education Plan reads: "All students and teachers will have access to information technology in their classrooms, schools, communities, and homes" (U.S. Department of Education, 2000a). This means that establishing good network management plans and procedures must be a priority for all technology coordinators. By setting up quality network access, making sure the network is properly managed and administered, and providing the support and training necessary for all users, the technology coordinator can ensure that students, teachers, and other staff members have the resources they need to work and learn in our networked world.

Schools have made considerable progress with the implementation of networking projects and Internet accessibility to teachers, students, and staff. The E-Rate program has been a critical factor in this progress. The funds provided to schools by this program have allowed virtually all schools to be connected to the Internet. It has also allowed many schools to develop the network infrastructure necessary to deliver this access to classrooms. The development of "a comprehensive infrastructure for learning when and where they need it" is one of the goals of the most recent updates to the National Education Technology Plan, released in draft form for comment and revision in early 2010 (U.S. Department of Education, 2010, p. xix).

The National Education Technology Plan was instrumental in the building of infrastructure, the creation of Internet access, and the pioneering of ways in which digital content and networked applications could be used to transform teaching and learning. Both the early National Education Technology Plans of 1999 and 2000, as well as the No Child Left Behind Act (NCLB) of 2001, had implications for educational technology policy. NCLB charges the U.S. secretary of education with the development of an updated National Education Technology Plan for education. The 2010 version of the plan establishes a national strategy supporting the effective use of technology to improve student academic achievement and prepare students for life and work in the

21st century. The development of this plan provides an opportunity to reflect on the progress made in connecting classrooms to the Internet during a decade of increased federal, state, local, and private investments. The Office of Educational Technology is developing this plan in conjunction with several organizations. More information about the plan can be found at www.ed.gov/technology/netp-2010.

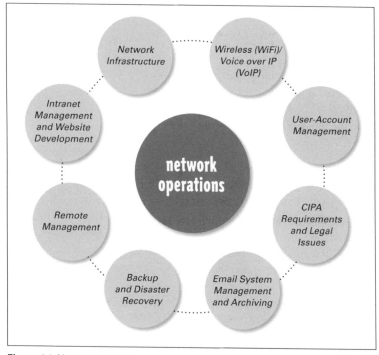

Figure 4.1 Network operations issues

Network Infrastructure

The success of a school computer network is dependent on the design and durability of its infrastructure. The wiring, *patch panels,* file servers, *hubs, routers, print servers, high-speed communications lines* (such as *T1, T3,* frame-relay, and *fiber-optic lines*), wireless devices, and other parts of the network system must work together seamlessly.

A poorly designed or maintained network will always fail at the worst possible moments.

Dealing with network infrastructure issues often requires highly specialized and advanced technical skills and knowledge. The technology coordinator may not be trained in all areas, but the coordinator should be willing and able to learn about them. This knowledge allows the technology coordinator to plan and implement an effective network infrastructure and manage installations and upgrades. A school's or district's technology plan should include a detailed analysis of network resource needs and methods for developing, expanding, and improving the infrastructure. The tech coordinator should work with school or district staff and the board of education, as well as outside vendors and consultants, to develop a network plan that will meet current and future curricular and administrative needs.

It is also important to plan for and secure adequate technical assistance for network equipment. A single person may not be able to handle server administration, user account setup, personnel training, equipment failures, and all the other requirements of network management. As a school's or district's network becomes more complex, the technology coordinator may need to work with administration to hire a certified network administrator: "The technology coordinator cannot do it all. Districts that have hired them and then become disillusioned because this person cannot oversee the whole thing, fix the problems, and train the staff—there just aren't enough hours in the day" (Reilly, 1999). If the technology coordinator is the only person in the district responsible for technology, a plan must be in place for handling routine network maintenance and for repairing critical components when they develop problems or experience failure. A variety of service and support contracts are available from vendors.

Significant investment in technology infrastructure, often thanks to the E-Rate program, allows many schools to install local area network (LAN) capabilities. Some technology coordinators, at times, must design, install, and configure networks for their districts or particular buildings, or expand the capabilities of an existing network. A tech coordinator who is planning to install or expand a network will face a variety of issues and decisions. Because the networking needs of each

helpful hint

Tech Support

If additional technical support for a school's or district's network infrastructure is needed, implementing the following items can help secure that support:

- Create partnerships with local businesses that have technical staff positions.

- Tap the expertise of the staff of local colleges.

- Contract with local vendors for regular and emergency technical support visits.

- Work with existing custodial and maintenance staff to provide assistance as needed.

- Provide technical training for existing staff or hire additional staff with specialized technical training.

- Make use of parent volunteers who work in technical fields.

- Solicit help from a local technical school's computer-repair program.

- Recruit student helpers. They may have unexpected technical expertise and be able to provide useful assistance.

organization are different, a network installed in one location may be quite different from that of another location, even in the same district.

One of the first tasks that a technology coordinator must perform is determining the type of network to be installed. At one time, the only choice for installing network capabilities was to run wire to all endpoint locations—essentially creating a hardwired network much like that of the telephone system. This method requires installing copper wire and connecting all the different endpoints with a central location where the central network equipment (servers, routers, and switches) is installed. Today, other, more cost-effective options exist. Installation of fiber optic cable may be an attractive option if large amounts of bandwidth are needed. Another option is the installation of a wireless network (*WiFi*) that connects devices to the network using only wireless access points.

Regardless of the network type, it is critical that a technology coordinator work with experienced technical experts to design and install the most appropriate network for a certain location. Some expertise may be available from staff with networking experience. Most schools, however, will need to engage contractors. These contractors will work with the technology coordinator and other technical staff to design and install the network.

For most schools, the LAN located in a school building will be connected to a larger network, either the district *wide area network* (WAN) or the Internet. When choosing how the school network will be connected to the outside world, the technology coordinator faces a variety of high-speed connectivity choices and issues. Schools can be connected through ISDN, T1, T3, *broadband* cable connections, or fiber optics. Each of these connection types has different speeds and costs.

ISDN connection. This digital transmission technology supports voice, video, and data communications applications over regular telephone lines capable of speeds from 57.6k to 128k. Integrated Services Digital Network is a telecommunications standard.

T1 connection. This type of digital data connection can pass data at a rate of 1.544 megabits per second.

T3 connection. This type of digital data connection can pass data at a rate of 44 megabits per second. T3 lines are often used to link large computer networks, such as those that make up the Internet.

Broadband cable connection. This type of digital data connection, provided by a cable company, can reach speeds of up to 33 megabits per second.

Fiber-optic connection. This connection via a thin strand of glass that carries light transmissions is used for high-speed voice or data transmission. Fiber-optic connections can support 30,000 times the traffic that can be carried on copper wire.

Several factors need consideration when determining the connectivity scheme for an organization or site. The first consideration is the number of potential connections. The second consideration is what types of services will be delivered over the network. For example, a site that will be accessing video-on-demand services will need higher capacity and connection speeds than a site that will be sending email and browsing web pages. The available budget is a third factor to consider. Finally, the types of connections actually available must be determined because connectivity service may vary by location.

To determine the best service option for providing network connectivity, it will be important for the technology coordinator to consult with the district's administration and business operations staff, network services vendors, network design consultants, and other stakeholders.

Tech Leader Profile 5

Pamela McLeod, Director of Technology

Pamela McLeod is the director of technology for Alton School District in Alton, New Hampshire. Alton is a rural community of around 4,500 in east-central New Hampshire, just south of the White Mountains and near the shore of Lake Winnipesaukee, New Hampshire's largest freshwater lake. This school district is made up of a single, K–8 school that has a student population of 620 and a separate district office known as a School Administrative Unit (SAU). She has spent the last four years in this position and is trained as an engineer in the IT field.

Pam earned an MS degree in engineering and reports to both the school principal and the district superintendent in her position. Although she does not currently hold any licensure or certification for technology leadership, Pam is working towards a licensure as a teacher. She supervises one other person in the technology department for Alton Central School. Her main responsibilities as technology director are administration of the school technology systems, management duties such as budgets and technology planning, and support of educational technology for the district. One of the challenges of a technology leadership position in a small organization is the wide variety of responsibilities one faces on a daily basis. Still, as Pam points out, this is also one of the things that she enjoys most about the position—each day brings a new challenge. Pam's tip for other technology leaders is "Be a good manager and planner in your leadership position; it is not enough just to be a technology geek."

Wireless Network (WiFi) and Voice over IP (VoIP) Technologies

Today, it is possible to create an essentially wireless network by installing a minimum of wired connections throughout a building and then installing wireless access points that allow computers to connect to the network using radio frequencies. These wireless networks have become more reliable, faster, and less expensive in the last several years, and their capabilities and speed continue to improve. In certain cases, this solution may be a better choice than a hardwired network. In a newer building with false ceilings and easy access to conduits in walls, it may be possible to install a copper wire network with minimal intrusion and nominal expense. In older buildings that have solid ceilings, it may be much more difficult and expensive to install a wire-based network throughout the building. The installation of a wireless network may be a better choice in such a location.

Many schools are using wireless networks to offer connectivity to teachers and students throughout the school building and in key locations around the school campus. According to Market Data Retrieval, some 10% of schools reported using wireless networks in 2001, but by 2005 that number had increased to 45% (Borja, 2006). That number has continued to increase, in many cases driven by the implementation of the 1-to-1 laptop initiative project. The National Center for Educational Statistics, in their fall 2008 report on educational technology in the public schools, noted that 78% of schools reported the availability of wireless networks in some part of the school building (Gray, Thomas, & Lewis, 2010). In addition to allowing connections from virtually anywhere, wireless networks make possible the connection of a variety of different devices. Students and faculty can connect to the network with laptops, *netbooks,* tablet computers, or smartphones. The adoption of wireless network capabilities makes it possible to simplify the lives of teachers and students.

A technology coordinator must consider a variety of issues when implementing a wireless network. A tech coordinator must take steps to ensure that wireless connections are secure and that unauthorized users cannot make use of the connections. It is also important to make certain the network access points are carefully placed throughout a building to avoid interference and assure there are no gaps in the coverage area. For complete coverage of a school building, numerous access points will be necessary, and the ability to easily manage these devices should be a consideration. Careful planning should be used when designing, installing, and implementing these systems.

Schools are also beginning to use their data networks to handle other types of communication, such as telephone calls. In an effort to save money, schools have begun to install telephone systems that use Voice over Internet Protocol, or *VoIP*, to handle calls. VoIP uses the existing infrastructure of computer data lines to route phone calls within a building or across the school district. Districts can sometimes realize considerable savings from implementation of VoIP systems. Keith Seher, an information manager for the 10,000-student David Douglas district in Portland, Oregon, estimates his district saved about $70,000 the first year it used the local area network already in place instead of local telephone lines (Davis, 2009).

There are a variety of issues that must be considered when implementing VoIP systems. A primary consideration is emergency backup. If, for some reason, the data system goes down, the phone system goes down as well. To accommodate emergencies, many schools continue to have at least one traditional analog phone line running into the building to handle calls. Cost is another factor that technology leaders should consider when investigating a VoIP solution. Some school districts do not have the wiring capability or the desire to switch all district calls to VoIP at once. It is also important to consider that analog phones can cost only about $12 each, compared with the smarter phones for a VoIP system, which can cost many times that amount.

If a district is considering the installation of a VoIP system, it is important for the technology coordinator to consider a variety of issues:

- Does the district have the appropriate network capacity to handle the data demands of district users, as well as the added capacity necessary to provide voice services?

- Does the district have the technical expertise needed to manage the new system?

- Will the potential savings in service costs be offset by the cost of the new system and the increased technical demands and support necessary from district staff?

It is important for the technology coordinator to work with district administration, technical staff, and vendors to carefully answer these questions when such an investment is being considered. Ultimately, any change to the phone system should not result in diminished or frustrating service for district phone users.

User-Account Management

The success of any network is best measured by the end users' level of satisfaction and productivity. A network's infrastructure may be of the highest quality, but if users have difficulty using the resources available, the network will not be viewed as a good investment of limited technology dollars. A user who is unable to log onto the network cannot access stored files, use network programs, visit a website, send an email message, or make use of a network printer. Problems with user accounts could cause a teacher who is uncomfortable with technology to abandon the network altogether—and lose all the many benefits it can offer. Effective management of user accounts is, therefore, crucial to network operations.

Although technology coordinators may not be directly responsible for user-account management, it is important that they establish standard procedures and understand related issues for typical user-account problems, such as how to access accounts for new users, whom to contact when questions and problems arise, what to do when a password is forgotten, and how to help users access network resources that are of most use to them. These procedures should be specified and communicated to all users of the network so that when questions and problems arise these users know what to do.

New account requests and problems with passwords are part of the day-to-day management of any network. At the beginning of a school year it may be useful to work with administration and school offices to develop a list of new staff members who will need user accounts. These lists should serve as the basis for new account requests. Lists of employees who have left the organization should also be developed so that those accounts can be removed. Password problems can arise at any time and need to be dealt with in a timely manner. Often these problems can be solved quickly by simply resetting a password that has been forgotten. It will be helpful for the technology coordinator or network administrator to designate a contact who can assist with these routine questions and problems. This person might be given some extra training and the authority to create new accounts and reset passwords as necessary.

Training new network users is a critical aspect of the technology coordinator's job. Technology coordinators who provide a mandatory introductory class ensure that all new users receive a standard introduction to network use. This class can be offered at a variety of times and locations at the beginning of the school year. The session can be quite basic in nature and can be taught by the technology coordinator or technology contacts at school sites.

This mandatory class can be a useful way to help people learn how to connect to the network with a user ID and password. A formal introduction to the network helps new users understand how the network is organized. This training can show new users such items as public versus private storage of files, and can help them learn what programs are available through the network, how to access such resources as the online library catalog, how to find out whom they can turn to when questions or problems arise, and so forth. This introductory class is also an ideal forum for introducing new users to the district's acceptable use policy (AUP).

Acceptable use policies are documents that outline the district's intended uses of the network and Internet. They set forth proper online behavior for users. A district's AUP should be one of the first policies developed when establishing a network and Internet connection. The technology coordinator is usually the staff member who is charged with formulating, implementing, and communicating this policy to other district staff.

Including the AUP in student handbooks ensures that all students and families have a copy of the document and, therefore, the opportunity to review it before school activities begin. By having a document that is distributed to every user, the technology coordinator can educate users on potential pitfalls and provide guidance for students and parents. Some schools choose to have the AUP signed by both students and parents and kept on file in the office or classroom. This may be a difficult task for a large organization, but such efforts provide long term benefits because this document defines boundaries of behavior and, more critically, specifies the consequences of violating those boundaries.

The following links provide helpful AUP guidelines and examples.

- Sample Acceptable Use Agreements and Policies from the National Center for Education Statistics: http://nces.ed.gov/pubs2005/tech_suite/app_a.asp

- AUP Information and Resources from the Virginia Department of Education: www.doe.virginia.gov/support/safety_crisis_management/internet_safety/acceptable_use_policy.shtml

- Guidelines for Creating Acceptable Use Policies from the Kentucky Department of Education: www.education.ky.gov/kde/administrative+resources/technology/additional+technology+resources/acceptable+use+policy+guidelines+and+state+requirements+for+student+and+staff+access+to+electronic+i.htm

- Acceptable Use Policies in the Web 2.0 and Mobile Era from the Consortium for School Networking: www.cosn.org/Default.aspx?tabid=8139

CIPA Requirements and Legal Issues

The Children's Internet Protection Act (CIPA) was passed by congress in December 2000. This act requires schools that receive federal funding for technology (such as E-Rate funds) to meet certain requirements. CIPA requires schools to enact Internet filtering to block obscene and pornographic materials in order to protect students from inappropriate materials. Schools are also required to enact an Internet safety policy. This policy must address several student access issues:

- Access by minors to inappropriate matter on the Internet

- The safety and security of minors when using electronic mail, chat rooms, social media, and other forms of direct electronic communications

- Unauthorized access including "hacking" and other unlawful online activities by minors

- Unauthorized disclosure, use, and dissemination of personal information regarding minors

- Restricting minors' access to materials harmful to minors

The act requires that the online activity of minors be monitored and that a public notice and hearing regarding the passage of the Internet safety policy be documented by the school or district. Schools applying for and receiving E-Rate funds must be prepared to document their compliance with the CIPA requirements.

A recent addition was made to these requirements with the passage of the Protecting Children in the 21st Century Act in 2008. This act requires schools receiving E-Rate funds to teach students about appropriate behavior on social networking and chat room websites, as well as the dangers of cyberbullying. To be sure that their policies are in compliance with all of these requirements, schools and districts should carefully review the acceptable use policies, Internet safety policies, and instructional plans to assure that all necessary requirements are met.

Tech Leader Profile 6

Jeremy Davis, Teacher for Instructional Technology

Jeremy Davis is a teacher on special assignment for instructional technology for the Magnolia School District in the western portion of Anaheim, California. The Magnolia School District serves 6,400 students in nine K–6 schools located in a suburban area of Anaheim, near Disneyland. Approximately 750 certified and classified staff members in the Magnolia School District serve the student population; nearly half are nonnative English speakers.

Jeremy has worked in this position for the past three and a half years. He reports to the assistant superintendent for student learning. After receiving a BA in psychology, Jeremy went on to earn an MBA in organizational leadership and eventually his teaching certification. He has been recognized as a Google Certified Teacher and has earned a State of California Certificate of Eligibility Administrative Services Credential. His main responsibilities are teaching model lessons that demonstrate the integration of technology in the classroom, developing technology curriculum for district schools, and conducting staff development sessions for district personnel. Jeremy works as part of a staff of three people in the Instructional Technology Department. In his professional capacity, working with the administration to effectively and financially provide the necessary level of technical support is the biggest challenge he faces on a daily basis.

Jeremy's tips for other technology leaders include learning to effectively use data to make your point and demonstrate your needs; taking advantage of resources like RSS feeds, social bookmarking sites (such as Diigo), and other professionals through social networking sites; getting involved with organizations (such as ISTE) that allow you to network with other professionals; helping district administrators see all the possibilities as they prepare to make decisions; standing firm in your convictions; and keeping your staff members excited about the possibilities technology holds for teachers and students.

Email System Management

A school or district email system is a vital network tool for all staff members. The email system makes it possible for individuals to communicate with other individuals and groups within the district; to send messages to parents, community members, and vendors; and to interface with others outside the district.

Effective management of the email system requires that procedures be established for creating new email accounts and removing unused accounts. Users must know whom to contact when problems arise with their email and where they can go to get assistance. A training program that covers how the system works, what features it provides, and how to make use of those capabilities is crucial for all users. Email systems today often provide a variety of features beyond the simple sending and receiving of messages, such as calendars for scheduling meetings, to-do lists, file sharing, and so forth.

In addition to sending emails to individuals, email systems offer the ability to send messages to groups. If an email system includes built-in group addressing, these addresses will need to be edited and updated as new people join a building or department and others leave. A school's or district's email address book must be updated on a regular basis, both to ensure accuracy and to limit user frustration. While this task may be carried out by a network administrator, the technology coordinator should work with the network administrator to ensure the accuracy of address book contents, coordinate communications with school administration regarding account management tasks, and coordinate training for new users.

When selecting an email system for use by the organization, the technology coordinator must be aware that every system has its pros and cons. Essentially, there are two basic types of systems available. An organization can either select a web-based email system (Yahoo! and Gmail are two examples of free web-based accounts) or an email system (such as Microsoft Outlook, Apple Mail, or Mozilla Thunderbird) that requires a local client. Although both systems serve the same purpose of sending and receiving messages, each has advantages and disadvantages.

Client-based systems use a program installed on a local computer to communicate with a mail server to send and receive messages. The advantages of using a client-based system include:

- Users have the ability to use as attachments a wide variety of file types.

- Users have a wider variety of email features, which are included as part of the client program.

- Users are able to store messages in folders on a local computer as well as in folders on the mail server.

The disadvantages of a client-based system include:

- Users will normally have to be working on their own computers in order to check their mail.

- The program will have to be configured before it will work with an individual user's account.

- The program is especially vulnerable to viruses.

Web-based email systems do not require a special email client to be installed; they can be accessed with a web browser such as Firefox or Internet Explorer. The advantages of a web-based system include:

- There is no need to do any special configuration.

- Mail accounts can be accessed from any computer that is connected to the Internet.

- The system often scans and filters incoming messages for viruses.

The disadvantages of a web-based system include:

- The system sometimes operates more slowly.

- File size for attachments is sometimes limited.

- The system sometimes does not include as many features as a client-based system.

- Files can only be stored in remote folders.

When dealing with email systems, technology coordinators should understand several protocols that are used in their operation. These protocols are Simple Mail Transfer Protocol (SMTP), Post Office Protocol (POP), and Internet Message Access Protocol (IMAP), each of which serves a different purpose.

SMTP is exclusively concerned with the sending of email between servers. This protocol is used for transferring email messages from one server to another over the Internet. The POP and IMAP protocols are concerned with the way in which email is retrieved from a mail server.

When using a POP-based system, messages are moved from the mail server to the local machine when the email client makes a connection. Once messages have been retrieved by the local machine, they are removed from the server. With an IMAP connection, the email is downloaded to the local machine, but a copy remains on the server. The advantages of the IMAP system is that messages remain on the server, can be accessed at a later time from another computer, and can be stored in folders on the remote system for easy access. To access a message retrieved from a POP system, the messages exist only on the computer that retrieved them, and the person must be using that computer in order to access the message at a later time.

The technology coordinator is not usually expected to be an expert on these different email protocols and system features. Still, a basic understanding is useful, because the coordinator will likely play an important role in making recommendations and decisions regarding a school's or district's email system. When it is time to make a decision about what options are best, or which system has advantages, the tech coordinator is often the individual who provides the information and understanding necessary to make an informed decision.

To maintain maximum system performance, the technology coordinator should create a schedule for conducting routine housekeeping tasks, such as managing user mailboxes. For example, some users tend to allow numerous messages to accumulate in their mailboxes, filling up considerable memory storage space on the email server. Limits should be set on the amount of mail that may be stored in an individual's personal mailbox. Creating appropriate policies—such as not using the system for solicitation, lobbying, or political purposes—and reminding users of these policies can help make the email system more efficient and, ultimately, more useful to staff members.

Although the technology coordinator may not be responsible for daily management of the email system, a good understanding of how the entire system works and of the capabilities offered is certainly necessary in order to train users and help them take full advantage of the system, which in turn results in satisfied users and a system that is easier to manage and maintain.

Email Archiving

A change in the Federal Rules of Civil Procedure in 2007 regarding electronic data *archives* created a new technology challenge for school districts. The new rules require that "electronic documents—including email and perhaps even instant messaging logs—be available as evidence in civil court cases" (Fonesca, 2007). This is a significant change with major implications for district technology operations. The rules require "companies, government agencies, school districts, and generally any organization that might be sued in federal court to have systems for retrieving electronic data such as email correspondence if it is needed as evidence in a federal case" (Davis, 2007). While email systems have always been part of regular network backup systems, these new requirements pose new technological challenges and may require investment in additional equipment and resources.

Although the new rules have established expectations for school districts, they are also somewhat unclear in the exact requirements that must be met. They require that districts preserve electronic documents that may be related to a case as soon as school officials have any indication that a lawsuit may be filed. In essence, the records must be preserved "in case of" a lawsuit. The rules also do not provide a clear timeline for keeping the records. While business records and student records must be maintained for a certain period of time, no time period is specified for electronic documents. The rules require the district set a reasonable policy for the maintenance of these records. Meeting the requirements of these rules may come with some expense for an organization. Significant storage capacity and additional equipment are often needed to maintain the archive of even a medium-sized school district.

Informal conversations with technology coordinators from across the country reveal a variety of responses to these new requirements. A California technology coordinator for a larger district had made significant investments in capacity in order to meet the requirements. Several Midwestern technology coordinators from small, rural districts have taken a wait-and-see stance. Other technology coordinators are moving toward the use of hosted email services such as Google Apps or Gaggle.net, which include *email archiving* as part of the package.

It is important for a technology coordinator to be aware of the revised archival requirements and work with district administration and board members to meet district compliance needs. It is also important for the technology coordinator to work with district leadership to institute a well-defined policy on email retention. In addition, the technology coordinator needs to work with technical staff to determine the volume of district email and what additional hardware and software are necessary for effective archival. If the district lacks the internal technical expertise to deal with the requirements, it may be best to work with a vendor that provides archiving services.

Backup Procedures and Disaster Recovery

One of the most important procedures for ensuring network stability and integrity is the regular backup of files and information that network users access and modify. When a network file server is installed, the network administrator and technology coordinator must develop and implement a comprehensive plan for the daily backup of critical information. They must ensure that the necessary backup equipment and software are installed and working properly. The backup plan should also include *disaster recovery procedures* to be used in the event of an attack on the system or its critical failure, so that vital data are not irretrievably lost.

Typically, files on the server are copied to tape in the early morning hours, when use of the system is minimal. After the backup is complete, the daily backup tape will need to be removed and stored, then replaced with the next day's tape. It is usually best to have a separate tape for each day of the business week. A designated person at each server location should be trained to switch the tapes on a daily basis.

As part of the disaster recovery plan, it is important to send a copy of the tapes to an off-site location each week. By locating a copy of the tapes off-site, a disaster such as flood or fire will not destroy all copies of important files. As new tapes are sent for off-site storage, the original tapes can go back into the pool for daily backup.

An essential part of the backup plan is training users to save copies of important data and other files to the file server so that they can be backed up. Most computers today have large quantities of local storage space, and users may not feel the need to store important files on the file server. Helping users understand the importance of backup and training them to make regular backups of critical information, such as grades, will help the backup plan succeed. Asking users to take a few minutes at the end of each work session to make a backup copy of important work will save later frustration. While computer equipment is often quite reliable, a single hard drive failure with no backup can lead to the loss of important documents and information.

Although technology coordinators may not be personally responsible for setting up

helpful hint

Network Backups

Users should be trained to store all their important documents on the network. By doing so, they can be assured that their information will be backed up on a daily basis. This information can also be accessed from any computer attached to the network. Storing files on a local hard drive limits access to the computer where the files are stored and does not guarantee the regular backup of the information. By training users in effective backup procedures, the technology coordinator helps users avoid losing critical data due to equipment failure or other unforeseen problems.

and managing the backup system, they can play an important role in ensuring that the system is working properly. The backup system and software should be monitored on a daily basis to make sure that important files have been backed up successfully, that the backup is complete before users arrive in the morning, and that an adequate supply of backup tapes is available as needed.

Remote Management

Management of a school district's network technology resources is a critical function that is usually handled by a small staff. Most districts have multiple servers, often located in different buildings (and even different communities), that must be serviced and supported by a small staff or a single individual. A server that goes down at a particular site may be miles away from an available technician, and the time necessary to drive to the site to provide support may result in lost learning time or office staff productivity.

A district with multiple servers in various locations should seriously consider acquiring the tools and resources necessary to allow remote management of servers and network equipment via the Internet. These tools provide a variety of resources to network administrators and technology coordinators who are responsible for maintaining the integrity of the network and keeping the servers up and running.

Remote management software tools for most types of network equipment are available from a variety of vendors. These tools allow a technician at a central location to monitor the operation of the network in multiple locations and report on the operating condition of devices such as servers, routers, and switches. When a problem is found with a piece of equipment, the technician is able to connect to the equipment from a remote site and take a variety of actions to resolve the problem. The technician may:

- Connect to the server console to complete diagnostics and access control software

- Reboot the server by recycling server power

- Recover or reinstall operating system software, applications, or user data

- Troubleshoot hardware problems

- Update drivers

- Install patches

- Manage rights, groups, and user accounts

The use of remote management software tools offers a variety of advantages to those organizations willing to implement them. First, they can reduce the need for technical staff to personally visit a site to resolve network problems. Also, before an actual system failure occurs, it is possible for support staff to identify hardware components that are experiencing performance problems. Such tools can also warn of an impending server problem before it happens, leading to fewer service interruptions.

Intranet Management and Website Development

One of the many challenges that faces an organization is effective communication. Communication is enhanced when computer networks are created and connected to the Internet. Users can share resources and information and collaborate with others. Schools that want their users to more effectively share and communicate information often establish websites and intranets. Websites contain information that is made available to the public, while intranets are essentially private websites that are usually restricted to internal users of an organization, such as the staff of a school district. The technology coordinator often plays a role in planning, establishing, developing, and managing district websites and intranets.

School districts often create private intranets to improve communication among staff. An intranet is one way to handle routine school administration issues and details. A private intranet available only to staff and teachers is an excellent place to publish such things as regulations, emergency procedures, human resources materials, and other relatively static information. A variety of paper-based forms can be published as files on the intranet and downloaded by district users. Publishing such forms on an intranet saves printing costs and allows information to be updated on a regular basis.

Because the technology coordinator is often the central figure in the establishment and maintenance of a district intranet, it is important the coordinator work with district administration and school leaders to answer questions regarding this technology. For example:

- What do we want to accomplish by establishing an intranet?

- Who are the intended users of the intranet?

- What resources do we need?

- How will we maintain it?

The last question on this list, how to maintain the intranet, is probably the most important for the technology coordinator. It is essential for stakeholders to determine the procedures for maintenance at the outset: who will be responsible, how often the site will be updated, and how these updates will be posted to the site. It may be decided that regular maintenance will be the responsibility of staff members in the departments publishing information on the intranet site. If so, the technology coordinator must be sure these staff members receive adequate training for making these updates and that they have the necessary software to complete the task.

By making sure regular maintenance of the site takes place, the district can be assured that important information is always up to date and readily available to employees.

One District's Success Story

This particular school district wanted to create a private intranet website to make district personnel information and forms accessible. Because the district already had a public website and server available, it created a new private intranet site on its public website and called it personnel.ourschool.org. The personnel page of the public website has a link to the intranet site. However, access to the intranet site requires users to enter a user name and password. An easy-to-remember user name and password were created and shared with all district staff. The new intranet website contains the following information:

- District personnel directory
- Work calendars for different employee groups
- Handbooks for different employee groups
- Insurance and benefit forms and information
- Certified staff salary schedule
- Miscellaneous payroll and leave forms

This district's intranet site is easy to access for any staff member, and the district saves on printing costs for a variety of information and forms. Moreover, it is easy for the department to update information and forms at any time. A simple intranet solution saved this district time and money and makes information easy to access by those who need it.

ANSWERS TO

Essential Questions

1. How can the technology coordinator ensure that the network infrastructure meets users' needs?

    The technology coordinator should work with administration and the board of education to create and carry out a network infrastructure plan that will meet the current and future needs of the school or district and achieve the goals of the technology plan.

2. What issues will confront the technology coordinator when providing Wireless (WiFi)/Voice over IP (VoIP) services to district users?

    The technology coordinator must be prepared to work with the network administrator to provide the necessary capacity and technical expertise needed by users of the district WiFi and VoIP services and equipment.

3. **How can the technology coordinator assist with the management of network user accounts?**

   The technology coordinator and the network administrator must work together to ensure that effective procedures are in place for managing network accounts and solving user problems. The technology coordinator must also plan and conduct training to help users understand the network and how to use it.

4. **What role should the technology coordinator play in helping the district to meet the legal requirements of the Children's Internet Protection Act (CIPA)?**

   The technology coordinator should work with the district administration and board of education to develop and put in place any policies and procedures required by CIPA.

5. **How can the technology coordinator assist with the management of the district email system, including archiving?**

   The technology coordinator's most important role here lies in training users to properly use the email system and effectively manage their own accounts. The technology coordinator should also work with the network administrator to ensure that that any required email archive of the district is maintained.

6. **How can the technology coordinator ensure that appropriate backup and disaster recovery procedures are regularly carried out?**

   The technology coordinator must work with the network administrator to ensure that a disaster recovery plan is in place, equipment and software are appropriate for regular backups, and the system is monitored regularly. Users must also be trained to follow appropriate backup procedures for important files and data.

7. **How can the technology coordinator use remote management tools to provide better network service and support?**

   The technology coordinator uses remote management tools to solve network-related problems in a timely fashion, often without a site visit. These tools are also used to constantly monitor the network, diagnosing potential problems that may diminish network performance or create service interruptions.

8. What role should the technology coordinator play in the development and management of the district intranet and public website?

The technology coordinator should take a lead role in the planning, establishment, implementation, and management of the district intranet and public website. The technology coordinator should also provide both the tools and training necessary for those who will regularly update the information on either or both of the sites.

Resources

Print Resources

Borja, R. (2006). Technology upgrades prompt schools to go wireless. *Education Week, 26*(9), 10–11.

Brown, R. (1999). *Serving six institutions: A history of administrative computing at the Associated Colleges of Central Kansas.* McPherson, KS: Associated Colleges of Central Kansas. (ERIC Document Reproduction Service No. ED444414)

Davis, M. (2007). Revised federal archiving rules raise legal, logistical challenges. *Education Week Digital Directions, 1*(3), 12–15.

Davis, M. (2009). Districts dial into the internet to modernize phone systems. *Education Week Digital Directions, 2*(3), 18–21.

Harrington-Leuker, D. (2001). *New networks, old problems: Technology in urban schools.* Washington, DC: Education Writers Association Special Report. (ERIC Document Reproduction Service No. ED456188)

Hovenic, G. (1997). *Log on to the future: One school's success story.* Des Moines, IA: Iowa State Department of Education. (ERIC Document Reproduction Service No. ED419518)

Jensen, D. (2000). Creating technology infrastructures in a rural school district: A partnership approach. In S. DeWees & P. Hammer (Eds.), *Improving rural school facilities* (pp. 57–69). Collected papers presented at the National Working Conference on Improving Rural School Facilities, Kansas City, MO. (ERIC Document Reproduction Service No. ED445859)

Lamont, B. (1996). *A guide to networking a K–12 school district.* (Unpublished master's thesis). University of Illinois, Urbana-Champaign.

Manzo, K. (2010). Digital innovation outpaces E-Rate policies. *Education Week, 29*(20), 1, 16.

New Mexico State Department of Education. (1995). *Educational technology institute report.* Santa Fe, NM: Author. (ERIC Document Reproduction Service No. ED460673)

Rogers, A. (1996). Living in the global village. *Electronic Learning, 13*(8), 28–29.

Son, T. (1998). *Network technology based application.* Portland, OR: Northwest Regional Educational Lab. (ERIC Document Reproduction Service No. ED417707)

Online Resources

Cisco Support and Downloads: www.cisco.com/cisco/web/support

Consortium for School Networking: www.cosn.org

An Educator's Guide to School Networks (Florida Center for Instructional Technology): http://fcit.coedu.usf.edu/network

Fonesca, B. (2007) E-discovery rules add summer IT work for schools. *Computerworld.* Retrieved June 20, 2010, from www.computerworld.com/s/article/print/9024018

Gray, L., Thomas, N., & Lewis, L. (2010). *Educational technology in U.S. public schools: Fall 2008* (NCES 2010-034). U.S. Department of Education, National Center for Education Statistics. Washington, DC: U.S. Government Printing Office. Retrieved May 15, 2010, from nces.ed.gov/pubsearch/pubsinfo.asp?pubid=2010034

Microsoft Product Support Services: http://support.microsoft.com

Novell Customer Support: www.novell.com/support

Reilly, R. (1999). The technology coordinator: Curriculum leader or electronic janitor? *Multimedia Schools, 6*(3). Retrieved May 24, 2000, from www.umass.edu/ednet/janitor.html

U.S. Department of Education. (2000a). *e-Learning: Putting a world class education at the fingertips of all children.* Retrieved November 22, 2001, from www2.ed.gov/about/offices/list/os/technology/reports/e-learning.pdf

U.S. Department of Education. (2000b). *Falling through the net: Toward digital inclusion.* Retrieved December 13, 2001, from http://search.ntia.doc.gov/pdf/fttn00.pdf

U.S. Department of Education. (2000c). *The power of the internet for learning: From promise to practice.* Retrieved December 20, 2001, from www2.ed.gov/offices/AC/WBEC/FinalReport

U.S. Department of Education. (2010). *National educational technology plan 2010.* Retrieved June 22, 2010, from www.ed.gov/technology/netp-2010

chapter 5

administrative computing

Essential Questions

1. What must the technology coordinator know about the selection, implementation, and support of the student information system for the processing of grades and attendance data, as well as other student records and information?

2. What is data-driven decision making and how can the technology coordinator support district personnel in this process?

3. How can the technology coordinator assist with the management of human resources information?

4. How can the technology coordinator ensure that administrators have the technology resources they need to manage the school's or district's business operations?

5. What issues must the technology coordinator consider when implementing and supporting a system for document imaging and management?

While a school district is primarily concerned with teaching and learning, it is nonetheless a business organization. In terms of technology, a school district must then use technology to manage and streamline its business operations. This type of technology, called administrative computing, includes information management and data processing systems and software programs. The technology coordinator has an important role to play in the administrative computing operations of the district.

Figure 5.1 Administrative computing issues

Schools and districts use administrative computing software in a number of ways. They use it to create and manage student records, set up master course schedules, enroll students in those courses, gather and analyze data about students in order to guide instructional decision making, and develop systems for keeping personnel and business records. Administrative computing software can help schools in the district handle a variety of information processing and distribution needs, from the purchasing of classroom textbooks and supplies to the management of menus, meals, and other food service provisions.

Technology coordinators should be prepared to understand and assist with these administrative computing needs. The coordinator will work with administrators and office staff to develop technology solutions, consult with vendors about available products, and conduct professional development training sessions for business software users. Through involvement in these activities, the tech coordinator can have a positive impact on the efficiency of a school's or district's business operations: "A well-planned information system in a school district significantly improves the ability of stakeholders to access data and efficiently make decisions" (Rodriguez, 1997).

Tech Leader Profile 7

Gordon K. Dahlby, Director of Curriculum and Technology

Gordon K. Dahlby is the director of curriculum and technology for the West Des Moines Community School District in Iowa. West Des Moines is a suburban school district serving 8,800 students. The district is made up of 14 schools, including nine elementary schools, two junior high schools, one 9th grade high school, one 10th–12th grade high school, and one 9th–12th grade alternative school.

Gordon has served in this position for 19 years. In this position, he reports to the associate superintendent of curriculum. In the West Des Moines schools organization, a director of technology is responsible for the technical side of the operation and reports directly to the superintendent. Originally trained as a secondary science teacher, Gordon earned a MS in school computer studies and a PhD in educational leadership and policy studies. He is licensed by the state of Iowa as a secondary school administrator. Gordon is part of a technology department made up of the two directors, four technicians, a database administrator, a network engineer, and a half-time staff development position. In the past, his position focused on technology planning, staff development, and equipment purchasing. Since the hiring of the director of technology, Gordon focuses his efforts on online learning environments and multimedia.

The biggest technology leadership challenge he faces on a daily basis is ensuring that technology supports teaching and learning. He points out that it is often easy to get caught up in boxes and wires and, hence, lose focus on supporting the curriculum. Gordon notes that while office productivity and data processing are important, the focus of technology efforts must be on the students. Gordon's tips for other technology leaders are: "It is essential to develop online tools that allow all teachers to communicate with students, parents, and the community—email, web pages, blogs, and podcasts all help with marketing and keep students and parents involved and supportive. Be sure to model the use of technology in staff meetings, parents meetings, and other gatherings. And, don't forget to celebrate and brag about the good things that are happening."

Processing Grades and Student Records

Managing and processing everyday school data such as grades, student and employee records, and payroll figures are common administrative computing tasks. This data processing occurs routinely in all schools and districts, and managing both the necessary technology and the related processes is a recursive task for technology coordinators.

An administrative information system revolves around the management of many different types of records. A variety of records are created for every employee who works for the district and for every student who is served by the district. These records need to be created, updated, and archived on a regular basis. The technology coordinator should work with administration to implement a system that adequately meets teachers' and administrators' data creation, collection, and reporting needs.

A centralized system usually offers advantages to a school or district with multiple buildings. By implementing a centralized system, student and employee records can be kept and maintained in one location, but they can be easily accessed by users throughout the organization. When a record is updated, the update is immediately available to all users of the system. If a school is using an information system that maintains records in separate locations, it is important to make sure all records are updated simultaneously so that current information is available to everyone.

Student Information Systems

The processing of data concerning grades is an ongoing administrative computing function. Student information systems often include a component for managing grade information for transcripts and other student records. At one time, the most common method for entering grade data was scanning bubble sheets that had been filled out by teachers. Computerized grading and attendance programs have become integral parts of student information systems, used to manage the daily information necessary to track student attendance and progress. Accurate and up-to-date information is available to teachers, administrators, and parents, thanks to these systems.

According to the Department of Education National Educational Technology Trends Study (NETTS; Bakia, Yang, & Mitchell, 2008) on the use of technology to manage student information, as of the 2006–07 academic year nearly all school districts maintained at least some school data electronically. This data often includes information about students: family information, courses taken, special program participation, immunization records, attendance, assessments, and grades. A comprehensive student information system allows stakeholders to facilitate communication and make effective decisions. The No Child Left Behind legislation requires districts to gather and manage large amounts of student information, with the assumption that this data would lead to positive changes in instructional practices.

Numerous student information systems have been developed by vendors for the K–12 educational market. Although some differences exist from product to product, certain basic features are included in all of them. A student information system should have the following basic features so that a school district can effectively manage student data.

Student records. The ability to store information about each student enrolled in the district, such as address, phone number, name of guardian, emergency contact, and so forth.

Master schedule. The ability to create a master plan of classes and sections offered by a school.

Individual scheduling. The ability to enroll students in particular classes based on a master schedule developed by the school.

Grade reporting and records. The ability to create progress reports, grading-period reports, and transcripts.

Attendance. The ability to provide student and class attendance records needed for state reporting by the school or district.

Reporting. The ability to generate a variety of reports based on the data in the system. With the increased requirements of the No Child Left Behind Act, this feature should be robust and provide a great deal of flexibility.

toolbox tip

Master Family Record

Establishing a master family record in the administrative information system ensures that information about several students from the same family is updated at the same time. This family record should contain all the basic information about the family: address, phone number, name of guardian, emergency contact, and so forth. When information is updated in the master record, all individual student records for that family are simultaneously updated.

Student information systems can have a variety of other features and add-on components. These features include the ability to post, on a protected website, assignment information and grades. Parents and students can log on to these protected sites and view the data. Some vendors include this feature as a standard part of their student information system. Other vendors make such features and capabilities available as an add-on component. Regardless, a growing number of schools are using this feature.

Other student information system features, or add-on packages and components, include special-education record keeping and IEP tracking, fee management, and textbook rental and inventory tracking. Additional products can be purchased to work in conjunction with the student information system to provide teachers with aggregated assessment information. These products can provide teachers with assistance for tracking standards and indicators.

All of these features, and often many others, can be found in programs such as PowerSchool or Chancery SMS, both of which are student information system products available from Pearson, a major player in the field of education products and publishing. PowerSchool is designed for use by small- to medium-sized school districts. Chancery SMS is intended for use by large, urban districts. Both products were originally developed by other vendors and have been acquired by the Pearson brand (www.pearsonschoolsystems.com/products). Other student information systems include Aeries from Eagle Software (www.aeries.com), Schoolmaster from Tyler Technologies (www.schoolmaster.com), or Infinite Campus (www.infinitecampus.com).

When selecting a student information system and a grade management program for district use, the technology coordinator, IT staff, administration, and project planning committee should make sure the system meets the needs of the organization. This selection process should include an analysis of the features the organization needs at the present as well as the future. If online access is planned, allowing students and parents to log on to a protected website to view grade and assignment information, careful attention should be paid to data security, equipment requirements, and teacher concerns about privacy. While such a system may make it possible to post student scores and grade data on the Internet, this can lead to the unreasonable expectation that this information should be posted immediately, which is not always possible or even desirable. Therefore, such a feature should be implemented only after weighing the pros and cons and after appropriate administrative policies have been developed and put into place.

The technology coordinator plays an important role in training users to implement the student information system. Users need to understand how the system works and how they can use it to perform their jobs more effectively. They must know how to get assistance when they have questions or encounter problems. Although the system may be maintained by IT staff or supported by outside vendors, the tech coordinator must serve as the local contact so that staff members have ready access to the data and information they need for quality decision making: "Those districts willing to take the plunge to build sustainable information-management systems are likely to reap many benefits" (Rodriguez, 1997).

Data-Driven Decision Making

Making instructional decisions based on the necessary data to support those decisions is a common part of the school improvement process. The data-driven decision making process occurs when teachers and administrators base educational decisions on the analysis of gathered student and program data. This data informs and guides the decisions necessary to improve student performance and school success. The Department of Education National Educational Technology Trends Survey (NETTS; Bakia, et al.) of 2008 revealed that access to electronic systems for gathering and managing student data increased from 48% in 2005 to 74% by 2007. As a result of the No Child Left Behind legislation and requirements, schools are collecting and analyzing more data than ever before.

Data from the school, district, and state levels is becoming more readily available (often electronically) and there is increased interest in using this data to make effective decisions. Teachers currently use existing student information systems to monitor student progress and to inform parents about student progress. The NETTS survey also indicates that while teachers may have some of the data analysis skills necessary for refining instructional practice, they would benefit from ongoing support and assistance. NETTS data reveal that teachers felt they would benefit from a process that allows them to use data more systematically and effectively.

The technology coordinator can play an essential role in the data-driven decision making process. Educational users of data (both teachers and administrators) need initial preparation and ongoing professional development in the use of the student information systems. The successful use of data for decision making purposes is not possible if staff members lack the skills necessary to organize and understand these data. The technology coordinator can partner with other district leaders, like school improvement leaders, district administration, and board of education members, to provide the preparation and training, support, capacity, and even the necessary time to analyze, interpret, and make decisions. These decisions can be instrumental in creating effective changes in instructional practice.

Tech Leader Profile 8

Karen Connaghan, Coordinator of Integrated Technology Services Division

Karen Connaghan is the coordinator of the Integrated Technology Services Division for the San Diego County Office of Education and the director of TechSETS, a California Department of Education statewide technology project. The San Diego County Office of Education provides services to 42 school districts made up of 298 individual schools in a largely urban setting. The county office also provides services to schools in suburban and rural settings. These schools serve a combined enrollment of more than 218,000 students. Karen has been working in this position for the past nine months and was previously director of technology at Kutztown Area School District in Kutztown, Pennsylvania.

Karen was originally trained as an elementary educator in Pennsylvania. She earned additional credentials in the following areas: instructional technology, reading specialist, K–12 administration, supervision of curriculum and instruction in Pennsylvania, and K–12 administration in the state of California. She holds a MA in educational technology from Pepperdine University and is currently pursuing a PhD in organizational leadership from that institution. The technology staff at the San Diego County Office of Education includes 60 staff members, six who are supervised by Karen. She reports to the assistant superintendent/chief technology officer in her organization. Her main responsibilities are providing resources, leadership, and training to technology professionals working in K–12 schools throughout the state of California; providing leadership, curriculum design, and coaching models related to educational technology and school reform for school districts in San Diego County; and collaborating with technical staff to ensure cohesive, integrated program design and project rollout.

Karen's biggest challenge is the management of the change process as she assists other professionals and school districts in making transformational changes to classroom learning. Her tip for technology leaders is that they must know and understand the culture of their organization. Some organization cultures are passive; some are aggressive; while others are facilitative. Knowing the culture informs professional developments, implementation needs, and human needs. This is critical knowledge when implementing and facilitating transformational change.

Human Resources

The management of human resources records is another area of administrative computing in which technology coordinators are likely to be involved. Information management systems used for student records can often be used for employee records, as well. This system can track such details as salaries, wages and hours, benefits, and supplemental contract agreements.

Technology coordinators can work with HR in the analysis and planning regarding technology purchases and implementation. The technology coordinator will then play a significant role in supporting the functions of a school's or district's human resources department. Coordinators can work with vendors to select the appropriate hardware and software, and they can provide training and ongoing support for users.

Implementing an HR information management system can be a complex and time-consuming undertaking. However, the benefits of a properly implemented system can be significant. Let's take a look at the procedures one school district followed to effectively implement a new electronic time clock system.

The district began by organizing a team made up of the technology coordinator, staff from district administration, and staff from the personnel and business offices. The team then reviewed current procedures and established project goals.

Team members found that current hourly record keeping was done on paper time cards. Every month, two payroll staffers spent 20 hours overtime apiece resolving and correcting time-card errors and questions. When processing yearly contract renewals, three people entered teacher contract information by hand in three different systems.

In meeting and reviewing this information, the team established goals for implementing an entirely new system. The most desirable system would use electronic time clocks to enter data directly into the payroll system. Contract information would be easily shared between different offices and systems that needed access to the data.

Once the goals for the project had been established, the technology coordinator contacted various vendors, providing them with a project description and requesting an informational product presentation. The team spent nearly six weeks viewing product demonstrations, comparing system features, and gathering additional information. The purpose of these informational sessions was to compare products and select several vendors from which to secure bids.

After the long list of possible products had been narrowed, the technology coordinator worked with the purchasing department to develop a request for proposals from vendors. The resulting document described the district project, outlined the project goals, and requested a proposal from each vendor that specified how the vendor might design a complete solution and the cost. Requests for proposals were sent to four of the vendors who had presented informational sessions. The team also spent time developing an evaluation process to help rate each proposal, including project scope, timeline for completion, how well the product met the project criteria, and the cost of the solution.

Each of the proposals was evaluated by the team according to the preestablished criteria. Ultimately, a single vendor was selected to provide the system and was contacted to meet with the team to begin detailed project planning. Timelines were developed and communicated to district schools and staff. The implementation of the electronic time clocks would be rolled out in phases, beginning with two sites and expanding, in phases, to all sites.

As the system was being installed at the district office site, initial user training took place for those who would directly use the new system to manage information on a daily basis. As the two pilot sites came online, various problems were discovered. Repairs and changes were made, and procedures were refined. As the district prepared to bring additional sites online with the time clocks, more users were trained to use the new system. Within a period of four months, all district sites were online.

After the completion of the project, the team continued to meet for several months to review progress and identify the benefits of the new system. Feedback from office employees indicated that processing hourly employee data for payroll no longer required overtime. Hourly employees indicated they liked having sick leave and vacation data available to them whenever they accessed the time clock system. Contract information now flowed much more efficiently between offices and systems.

In this case, the technology coordinator provided important leadership and assistance in facilitating a project to benefit district staff and improve the management of information. By using a simple seven-step process, problems with the current human resources system were addressed, and procedures improved, to the satisfaction of both the district staff and the employees. These seven steps were review, set goals, gather information, get proposals, plan project, implement carefully, and evaluate progress.

The technology coordinator can also assist with employee recruitment. A system can be implemented for posting job opportunities on the district's website and other employment websites. Postings can be placed with university placement offices. States offer online job listings as well, such as the Kansas Education Employment Board (www.kansasteachingjobs.com) and the Florida Department of Education (www.teachinflorida.com). National listings such as the

Clearinghouse for School Positions in the U.S.A. (www.wanttoteach. com) or the Regional Educational Applicant Placement website (www.reap.net) are also good places to post openings. By listing job opportunities on these sites, a school or district will have a better chance of hiring highly qualified candidates for open positions.

Business Operations

Purchasing is an important part of a school's or district's daily operations. The business office must generate purchase orders, track the filling of these orders, acknowledge the receipt of merchandise, manage the inventory of district assets, and arrange for the payment of accounts. In addition, a district is often required to generate requests for proposals and bids involving large purchases and then manage the bidding process to award contracts.

Although business officers usually manage these purchasing operations, the technology coordinator often plays a role in supporting the technology they use. This technology usually takes the form of a centralized information management system. Such a system may be an add-on component of the student information management system or it may be separate. Two examples of business operations systems are the alio School Business Management Solutions suite from Weidenhammer Systems Corporation (www.hammer.net/template. asp?nav_id=8) and the Isis Enterprise Management Solutions suite from Education Management Systems (www.k12financials.com). Both of these products include components to manage purchasing and receiving, fixed assets, and warehouse inventory.

It is the responsibility of the technology coordinator to ensure that appropriate technology resources—such as connectivity, workstations, and training for users of key programs—are available to business office staff. For example, to access the information management system effectively, all offices must have the necessary network connections. In addition, office staff who work eight hours a day with purchasing or accounting data may need workstations with high quality and larger sized computer monitors to help avoid eyestrain. Also, workers need to be trained in the daily operation of the workstation and software they use.

The effective use of technology to support the purchasing operations of a school or district will result in better financial management. An information management system enables the school or district to have better access to financial data and other critical information necessary for decision making. This system also allows for better use of available school resources.

Document Imaging and Management

School districts, like many other organizations, generate a huge amount of paper records as part of their day-to-day operations. Management of business records, student records, transcripts, student portfolios, required reports, and other paper documents is a major challenge for many schools and districts. Records must be maintained in accordance with state and federal law, as well as the record keeping and business needs of the school or district itself. The technology coordinator can help streamline this task by planning and implementing a system for document imaging and management.

Document imaging is the conversion of a paper document into an electronic image that can be accessed by a computer. After a document has been converted into an image and stored in the system, it can be retrieved quickly and efficiently. An imaging system is made up of several separate elements, all of them important. These elements include scanning, storage, retrieval, indexing (creating a system for document filing), and user access (see Figure 5.2).

When considering a document management system, a technology coordinator must consider two critical elements: storage and retrieval processes. Many different types of scanners are available, and they are capable of scanning anywhere from a few pages per minute to several hundred. As part of initial planning, conducting a careful needs analysis will help determine the number and types of scanners needed and where these scanners should be located. A variety of storage options are available. Most organizations will benefit from recording information on some kind of optical drive and using a jukebox device to distribute and arrange information on several different discs.

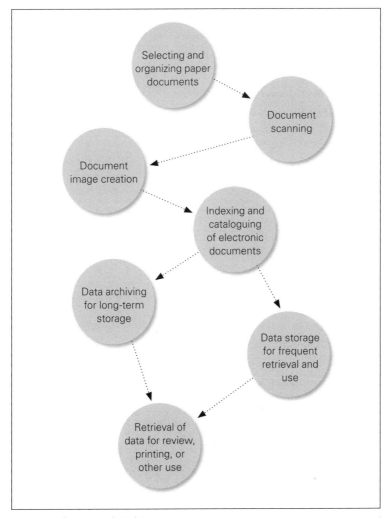

Figure 5.2 Document-imaging process

Document management software can be used to organize and index documents so that they can be retrieved easily. Documents can be indexed in several ways: fields and keywords indexing, full-text indexing, or a file or folder system. Good document management software allows information to be indexed in a variety of different ways at the same time so that users can easily retrieve needed information regardless of how they search for it. Some users may wish to retrieve information by keyword, while others need to find documents through the use of full-text searches.

The final component of the document-imaging system is control of access to the archived documents. This system must provide users with easy access to the information they need while, at the same time, restricting access to sensitive information that is not within their purview. Some users need access to student records, others to employee files, while still others need to access business records stored in the system. The system must be flexible enough to meet all these different needs without compromising security.

A variety of important questions must be asked when planning and establishing a document-imaging system that will meet a district's document management needs. Among them are the following:

- What problems will this system solve and how will the system improve the productivity of the organization?

- How many documents will the system store, and for what purpose?

- How many users will need to use the system at the same time?

- Which offices will need access to the system, and where are the users located?

- Is the necessary network connectivity available for users of the system? Is this connectivity adequate for the system's successful use?

For some districts, the planning, purchase, implementation, and support of a document imaging system will be a viable project. For others, the implementation of such a system may be out of the question due to budget constraints, lack of staff to install and support such a system, or limited return on investment due to the size of the district.

Outsourcing may be a possible solution for those districts that want to implement such a system but have limited resources. Outsourcing document imaging can provide electronic storage and access to information and documents while avoiding the up-front costs of acquiring and supporting such a system. This is a possibility that must be explored when considering the implementation of an imaging and management system for a district.

By working with administrators and office staff to determine the answers to the previous questions, the technology coordinator can design a document management system that meets user needs. The coordinator will then need to work with vendors to select the appropriate hardware and software, plan the installation of the system, create a training program for users, and address issues of system administration and ongoing support.

The successful planning and implementation of a document management system can have many benefits for a school district. Archived documents are more easily accessed by users, thus increasing productivity. Document access is more easily regulated, ensuring employee- and student-record confidentiality. Records are readily available precisely when they are needed. Principals, for example, can review employment applications on their personal computer rather than visiting the personnel office to review them. A document management system also saves considerable space in the storage of archival files, and electronic documents can become part of a disaster recovery plan. Archived records can be copied and stored off site to allow the re-creation of the data archive system should a disaster occur and destroy the paper records of the organization.

Although administrative computing may not be the chief focus of the technology coordinator's job, the leadership, support, and guidance that tech coordinators can bring to these activities will help ensure the success of the organization and maximize the return on investment in technology in support of a school's or district's business operations.

ANSWERS TO
Essential Questions

1. **What must the technology coordinator know about the selection, implementation, and support of the student information system for the processing of grades and attendance data as well as other student records and information?**

   The technology coordinator should have a detailed understanding of the system used to manage grades and student information in order to provide training, offer assistance, and give ongoing support to users of this system. All those who work with students and grades, as well as those who manage this data at the district level, will need this training and assistance.

2. **What is data-driven decision making and how can the technology coordinator support district personnel in this process?**

   Data-driven decision making is the process of getting student data (especially assessment and background data) into the hands of teachers, the primary instructional decision makers, for the purpose of planning and implementing strategies that will lead to increased student achievement. The technology coordinator plays an important role by providing the technology resources, professional development, and support necessary to help teachers make effective decisions based on the data available.

3. **How can the technology coordinator assist with the management of human resources information?**

   In addition to user support and training on the information management system, the technology coordinator should be prepared to assist with the posting of employment opportunities to various websites in order to attract quality teacher candidates and applicants for other positions.

4. **How can the technology coordinator ensure that administrators have the technology resources they need to manage the school's or district's business operations?**

   In supporting the purchasing process for a school or district, the technology coordinator must ensure that users have the workstations, software resources, network connectivity, training, and support they need to perform their jobs efficiently.

5. What issues must the technology coordinator consider when implementing and supporting a system for document imaging and management?

In implementing a system for document imaging and management, the technology coordinator must discuss the documentation needs and overall scope of the system with administrators and staff, work with vendors to select the appropriate hardware and software, and develop a comprehensive plan for successful training and support of system users.

Resources

Print Resources

Anderson, R., & Dexter, S. (2000). *School technology leadership: Incidence and impact.* (National Survey Report No. 6). Irvine, CA: Center for Research on Information Technology and Organizations. (ERIC Document Reproduction Service No. ED449786)

Carter, D. S., Kelly, P., & Connors, M. (1996). *Implementing an instructional information management system in a catholic secondary school.* Paper presented at the National Conference of the Australian College of Education, Perth, Australia. (ERIC Document Reproduction Service No. ED413632)

Conley, K. (Ed.) (2007). Student information systems buyer's guide. *Learning & Leading with Technology, 34*(4), 40–41.

Gallagher, L., Means, B., & Padilla, C. (2008). *Teachers' use of student data systems to improve instruction: 2005 to 2007.* Report prepared for the U.S. Department of Education. (ERIC Document Reproduction Service No. ED504214)

Hallman, T. (1995). *Getting everyone into the tent.* Association of Small Computer Users in Education Conference Proceedings, Myrtle Beach, SC. (ERIC Document Reproduction Service No. ED387098)

Hoffman, R. (2002). Strategic planning: Lessons learned from a "big-business" district. *Technology and Learning, 22*(10), 26–38.

House, J. E. (1989). *The impact of personal computing technology on the educational administration knowledge base.* Education Writers Association Special Report, Washington, DC. (ERIC Document Reproduction Service No. ED387895)

Ngoma, S. (2009). *An exploration of the effectiveness of SIS in managing student performance.* (ERIC Document Reproduction Service No. ED507625)

Online Resources

Clearinghouse for School Positions in the U.S.A.: www.wanttoteach.com

Electronic School (the e-zine of the National School Board Association's Technology Leadership Network): www.nsba.org/SecondaryMenu/TLN/TLN.aspx

ISTE National Educational Technology Standards for School Administrators: www.iste.org/standards/nets-for-administrators.aspx

Kansas Education Employment Board: www.kansasteachingjobs.com

Laserfiche Document Imaging and Management for K–12 Schools: www.laserfiche.com/en-us/Industry/School-Districts

Regional Educational Applicant Placement: www.reap.net

Student Information System Products from Pearson (PowerSchool and Chancery SMS): www.pearsonschoolsystems.com/products

State Educational Technology Directors Association—National Trends Reports 2004–2010: www.setda.org/web/guest/nationaltrends

Student Information Systems Demystified: www.techlearning.com/article/Student-Information-Systems-Demystified/45180

Teach in Florida (Florida's official teacher recruiting site): www.teachinflorida.com

chapter 6

planning
and budgeting

Essential Questions

1. What should the technology coordinator know about developing a comprehensive and successful technology plan?

2. How can the technology coordinator assist administrators in creating and carrying out a sound technology budget?

3. How can the technology coordinator assist in evaluating the effectiveness of technology use in the school or district?

4. What must the technology coordinator do to ensure proper licensing of software?

5. What must the technology coordinator do to make sure equipment is properly maintained, upgraded, and repaired as necessary?

6. What role should the technology coordinator play in the recycling and disposal of computer equipment?

7. What can the technology coordinator do to assist the district in hiring the appropriate IT staff?

8. What does the technology coordinator need to know about grant writing to locate and secure additional funding for technology projects?

9. What should the technology coordinator know about the E-Rate program and application process?

The primary function of a technology coordinator is to serve as the technology leader for the school or district. The importance and challenge of this leadership role are most evident in the areas of planning and budgeting.

The technology coordinator can best fulfill this role by articulating a vision for technology use in the school or district; establishing a clear, achievable plan for making that vision a reality; and working with administrators and the board of education to find the resources necessary to make it all happen. By developing a comprehensive and appropriate technology budget, securing grants and other outside funding to move big programs forward, and applying for discounts and refunds from the E-Rate program, the tech coordinator can have a tremendous impact on the successful implementation of technology in the school or district.

Figure 6.1 Planning and budgeting issues

Technology Planning

Over the past 30 years, schools have spent vast sums of money purchasing technology for classrooms and offices. While this spending shows a dramatic increase in technology investment, there has often been a lack of essential planning regarding what purposes the technology would serve and how it would be used to accomplish those purposes. The expectation has commonly been that simply placing technology tools in the classroom leads to exciting results and improved student learning.

However, any school or district that wants to make sure technology expenditures have the intended impact for students and staff must have a carefully developed technology plan. This plan represents a three- to five-year road map of where the school or district wishes to go with technology. It also represents the results of many conversations among board members, administrators, teaching staff, and people in the community regarding how technology can support the learning process. Consideration is given to how pedagogy and the learning environment must change in order to make better use of the available technology tools and, in so doing, provide richer experiences for students. The technology coordinator plays an important role in fostering and sustaining these conversations.

Most schools and districts today develop technology plans. In fact, districts are often required to submit a plan to the state for approval, particularly if E-Rate funding is involved. In order for a school to be eligible to receive E-Rate funding, its technology plan must have been approved by the state or some other organization charged with reviewing and approving such plans.

In the past, plans often concentrated on the acquisition of hardware or the development of network infrastructure. While these components are important, an effective technology plan encompasses much more. Barnett (2001) has defined 10 essential elements of a successful technology plan:

- Create a vision
- Involve all stakeholders

- Gather data

- Review the research

- Integrate technology into the curriculum

- Commit to professional development

- Ensure a sound infrastructure

- Allocate appropriate funding and budget

- Plan for ongoing assessment and monitoring

- Prepare for tomorrow

The previous list comprises the basic components necessary for the development of a technology plan.

It might be beneficial to consult some online resources before beginning the process of developing or updating a technology plan. For example, the National Center for Technology Planning provides a variety of models and approaches for planning technology. Founded by Larry Anderson in 1992, the National Center for Technology Planning (www.nctp.com) serves as a clearinghouse for information. The website makes available a wide range of plans from schools and districts across the nation. It also contains articles, brochures, checklists, and other items to assist in the planning process. While many of the resources on the site are free, the site does sell selected items, such as audiotapes and a guidebook. Other services include coaching, consulting, and workshops.

The technology coordinator needs to enlist the aid of a variety of stakeholders when beginning the planning process. By involving teachers, administrators, board members, community representatives, and students, a wide range of ideas can be expressed and vetted, and a broad base of support for the plan can be established. The coordinator should work with these stakeholders to develop a vision statement that defines what the technology program will look like in three to five years. The statement should include how students and teachers will be using technology to support and enhance the learning process.

Tech Leader Profile 9

Justin Hardman, Head of Educational Technology

Justin Hardman is the head of educational technology at Hong Kong International School in the Hong Kong Special Administrative Region of China. This private K–12 independent school serves more than 2,600 students with 480 faculty and staff working at four schools on two separate campuses. In this position, Justin reports to the high school principal. He has served in this position for the past two years. He works alongside the technology infrastructure support department with a staff of 16 and three other technology coordinators or facilitators in the other three academic divisions. Justin holds a bachelor's degree in economics but has no training in the education field.

Justin's main responsibilities are technology planning, leadership in educational technology systems, coordination of instructional technology resources, and technology integration. He identifies time management as one of the biggest challenges he faces on a daily basis. For him, it is a constant challenge not to get caught up in the small details of the day and to be able to delegate tasks effectively. Justin's tip for other technology leaders is, "You must be able to model the change you want to see in your teachers. If you do this well and teachers pick up on it, the students will too."

No planning process can be effective without data to support decision making. The technology coordinator must provide the planning group with up-to-date information about a school's or district's technology inventory, that is, the equipment and software currently used in classrooms, labs, and media centers. It is also a good idea for the technology coordinator to conduct a system-wide survey of technology usage by teachers and students and report the results to the group. Information about how other districts are making good use of technology can also be shared. Arranging site visits so that stakeholders can see how teachers and students in other schools use technology in novel and compelling ways is an excellent way to raise awareness and interest.

helpful hint

NETS

One way a technology coordinator can emphasize the importance of ongoing staff development for schools is to familiarize the planning committee with the National Educational Technology Standards (NETS) developed by the International Society for Technology in Education.

The NETS project developed standards for K–12 students, teachers, and administrators. Linking plans for professional development to the standards for teachers and administrators will result in more effective technology integration practices. More information about NETS can be found at www.iste.org/standards.

The technology planning committee will benefit immensely if members are given access to current research on the use of technology in learning. The technology coordinator should consider creating a summary review of the literature, identifying and locating articles that are particularly appropriate for the task at hand and sharing that information with the planning committee. By emphasizing current research on learning, the technology coordinator can help focus the committee's planning efforts. The focus should be on how to integrate technology more successfully into the curriculum rather than on hardware specifications, software titles, or network infrastructure. Powerful computers, the latest software, and high-speed access to the Internet are great, but they are not enough by themselves to ensure successful technology integration. Enhanced student learning should always come first when creating or revising a technology plan.

The allocation of resources for professional development and training is often missing from a school's or district's technology plan. While considerable attention is often paid to the purchase and upkeep of equipment, the need to train teachers and staff to effectively use that equipment is often overlooked—a critical mistake. The technology coordinator must be sure that an ongoing professional development program is integrated into the technology plan. Failure to include this element, or an emphasis on one-time-only opportunities for staff development, will make the success of the plan much more elusive. It is important to note that one of the changes required by the No Child Left Behind Act is an emphasis on long-term, sustained professional development in a variety of areas, including the use of technology for learning.

The technology plan must also address technical support and infrastructure needs. The technology coordinator is usually responsible for identifying those needs and drafting a budget that will support them in a stable and sustainable way. Too often, funding for these needs is haphazard, relying on funds left over at the end of the year or other "soft" money, such as grants. For some organizations, this practice has led to questionable purchasing decisions. By working with the board and administration, the tech coordinator can make sure necessary financial support is in place to carry out all components of the technology plan.

No technology plan is complete without an evaluation component: staff, teacher, and student use of technology must be regularly monitored and assessed for progress. The technology coordinator should assist in developing and administering surveys, defining learning outcomes, and implementing evaluation *rubrics* throughout the school or district. The information gathered from these assessments should be compiled and shared with stakeholders for further analysis and use in future planning. In order to stay on top of exciting new developments in technology that may improve learning outcomes, the tech coordinator should also regularly read about new products and developments, attend conference presentations, and discuss products with vendors.

As you can see, a technology plan is much more than a shopping list of hardware and software needs. It is a comprehensive plan that includes a variety of critical components that, taken together, "provide the necessary information to address not only technology but school improvement needs, and will provide the programmatic support necessary to sustain this project over time" (New York State Education Department, 1996).

Budgeting

Providing and supporting technology requires considerable financial commitment from a school district. In order for a technology program to be successful, the technology coordinator and administration must ensure that an adequate budget is available to provide all necessary equipment, software, connectivity, repairs, support, and training. While few businesses would ever try to implement a technology program without at least a minimal budget for it, school districts have been known to attempt to start them without identifying and obtaining adequate financial resources. The technology coordinator must make sure this does not happen; money must be allocated in each budget cycle for hardware, software, maintenance, telecommunications services, miscellaneous supplies, and professional development.

The technology coordinator can ensure that the school or district technology plan is suitably funded and sustained by budgeting carefully; assessing administrative, curricular, and infrastructure needs; and working with the board of education and administration to develop funding that adequately meets those needs.

Building an effective budget can be a time-consuming process for the technology coordinator. Considerable time can elapse from the initial needs assessment to the actual approval of a budget; therefore, the earlier the start, the better the outcome. While each district will have a budgeting process that is unique to that organization, some common themes can be recognized.

One of the first steps in the budgeting process is data collection and needs assessment. In this phase of the process the technology coordinator, usually working with the planning committee, gathers such data as inventory and professional development statistics, as well as any other information that provides a current picture of technology in the district. It is also useful for the technology coordinator to review the current technology plan to determine what progress has been made and how the plan is proceeding. In addition, it is important for the technology coordinator to communicate with district and building administration, curriculum committees, and other constituencies to identify perceived technology needs and wants throughout the district.

When data has been collected and a list of needs determined, the actual work on a preliminary budget can begin. This budget must provide resources in two general areas: an operations budget, which provides the funding to pay the ongoing costs of providing technology services and support, and a capital improvements budget, which provides the funds to purchase new technology resources and provides upgrades and improvements to existing ones.

toolbox tip

Allocation Formula

A successful technology budget will allocate dollars for a variety of different needs. A good plan contains an allocation formula that is appropriate for the needs of a school or district. Following is an example.

Hardware 35%

Software 15%

Contracts and services 10%

Professional development 20%

Support and maintenance 10%

Upgrades and other needs 10%

Specifically, operations funding includes the funds necessary to pay technology staff, provide Internet services, pay contract costs for support agreements and software licensing, purchase day-to-day repair parts, and provide professional development services. Capital costs are those associated with the purchase of new computers, servers, network equipment, replacement and upgrades to workstations, and such other hardware purchases as printers or projectors.

At this point in the process, the technology coordinator works with technology staff, administration, and other groups to identify specific areas of need. The coordinator will attempt to fit these needs into a workable budget plan. Part of the budget will be made up of fixed costs that will be ongoing, and so must be factored in first. Fixed costs include such items as salaries, network connectivity, and support contracts. Part of the budget will likely be devoted to equipment replacement and upgrades because machines eventually wear out and must be replaced. The final part of the budget will likely be made up of new initiatives that may be defined by the technology plan or advocated for by the administration. There may even be an initiative suggested by a building or group that advocates the implementation of something new. It is the responsibility of the tech coordinator to create a workable first draft of the budget by successfully balancing the specified needs and their costs.

After the first draft of the budget has been developed, the budget will usually be submitted to central administration for consideration. During the time all departments and units of the school district are in the process of developing draft budget proposals, a period of negotiation and revision will take place. The technology coordinator will need to work with central administration to help them understand the various elements that went into the draft budget proposal, including the needs outlined in the technology plans, targeted in the needs assessment, and expressed by the staff of schools or departments.

As budget negotiations continue, the technology budget, along with all other departmental and school budgets, will go through a process of revision. A considerable amount of give and take occurs during this period. Each department will have identified needs, wants, and goals for their budget. Their draft budgets will reflect these different goals, and there will be some level of competition for budget funding. Through negotiation and compromise the district must find a way to successfully balance the needs of all the departments while dealing with the realities of a limited budget. Given the current condition of the economy in most states and communities, few school boards are willing to levy tax increases in order to increase school budgets.

Following the negotiations with central administration and other departments, the final draft of the technology budget will be developed. The actual budget will be set by the local board of education, so it is important that the technology coordinator can justify the budget as presented and should, therefore, base budget requests on data that show the benefits of technology spending for the district. By beginning early, using data to determine need, developing a draft budget based on realistic expectations, considering the needs of others, and being willing to compromise, the tech coordinator can ensure that a successful technology budget is developed for the district.

Evaluation

Schools invest large sums to implement educational technology in classrooms. While it has been acceptable, up to now, to evaluate this investment either in terms of numbers of students per computer or level of Internet connectivity, school leaders increasingly must find ways to determine if this investment is paying off in terms of student learning. With the growing emphasis on school accountability, the ability to demonstrate the beneficial impact of educational technology has never been more important for schools. The development of assessment tools and techniques that reliably evaluate the effective use of technology in classrooms and staff rooms is a considerable challenge for the technology coordinator. Nonetheless, this process is crucial for demonstrating that the technology program is on track, and that modifications to the program are being made as necessary to better serve the needs of students, teachers, and staff.

As with any other part of the educational program, technology evaluation must be a systematic process. The technology coordinator must begin by identifying how the evaluation will be structured and what is to be learned from it. Assessment tools should be selected or developed based on the fundamental goals of a school's or district's technology plan. They may include surveys, interviews, observations, focus groups, checklists, paper-and-pencil or online instruments, and analysis of additional data such as standardized test scores or scores from state or local assessments. Many resources on technology evaluation and assessment can be found on the Internet. See the resources section at the end of this chapter for several useful tools.

After data have been collected from either existing sources or new assessments, the information must be analyzed in order to draw conclusions and make judgments about the program. The data collected during this process can be important in making long-range decisions about future technology purchases and initiatives. Assessment must be an ongoing process, of course, because technology and the way users employ it are always changing. The evaluation process must be continuously revised, modified, and adapted to successfully gauge performance and growth.

Assessment results should be shared with a variety of different audiences—the administration, the board of education, and the community. The technology coordinator should tailor the information to fit the particular needs of each of these groups. Doing so helps each group understand the importance of technology investment and the ways in which students benefit from this investment. Visual representations such as graphs and charts, for example, can be far more effective with a community group or the local board of education than can a long, detailed report or narrative. On the other hand, state departments of education may require a detailed narrative with plenty of data. It is important that a technology coordinator carefully consider the intended audience when planning this assessment report.

helpful hint

Branzburg Procedures

Branzburg (2001) offers a useful step-by-step list of procedures to consider when planning technology assessment:

- Discuss why you are evaluating.

- Determine specific questions you want to answer.

- Decide what data will help to answer your questions.

- Design the evaluation. Get help if necessary.

- Collect the data.

- Analyze the information collected.

- Share your results with others.

- Use the information to make effective decisions.

Meaningful technology assessment can offer a variety of benefits. Results from the assessment help demonstrate whether the technology program is making progress, determine if the investment has been worthwhile, and assist in making adjustments in the way the program is operating. The conversations that result from planning and implementing the assessment also help everyone involved to better understand the program and its focus. By offering leadership in this process, initiating the conversations, working with administrators and teachers to design or select assessments, and helping analyze and share the results, the technology coordinator can play a critical role in the continuous improvement of a school's or district's technology program.

Software Licensing and Installation

Although the installation and setup of equipment is important, this equipment is of little use without an operating system and software programs appropriate to the needs of end users. As discussed in Chapter 2, the technology coordinator is concerned with the selection, purchase, and installation of a standard set of programs for each computer. The selection of a software suite ensures that all users will have access to the same tools. Whether the user sits down to use a computer in a classroom, lab, library, or office, the same programs will be available on machines in each of these areas.

Several options exist for licensing these programs. Some organizations may choose to purchase equipment that includes the required software. The advantage in doing so allows capital outlay funds, which normally cannot be used for the purchase of software alone, to be used for this purchase. The result is a computer with preinstalled software that is rolled into the price of the machine. Alternatively, organizations may choose to license and install the programs separately from the equipment.

The choice an organization makes depends primarily on what software packages they wish to have installed on the machines and whether these packages are available as a standard option. If, for example, a district wishes to

helpful hint

Buying Consortiums

Software costs are a challenge for any school or district. An effective way to reduce licensing costs is to look for organizations or buying consortiums that allow the district to become part of larger purchasing blocs. For example, state contracts may offer opportunities for reducing software costs, particularly for common programs. Educational service centers may also offer programs to assist schools in this process. Service centers can use volume purchasing to secure a wide range of software packages at prices often unavailable elsewhere. Therefore, before buying from a commercial vendor, check pricing options available through a state contract purchase or a local educational service center.

have Microsoft Office installed as a standard package, and the software can be purchased already installed on a computer, then doing so will save the district installation time and allow it to use capital outlay dollars to make the purchase. If the district wishes to install a software package not available as a standard option, it may be necessary to either license the software separately and then install it, or set up a master machine and have the new equipment cloned. If the district chooses to install some of the many freeware or shareware programs available, then installation after delivery, or working with the vendor to have the machines cloned, are likely the only options.

In addition to looking at price options available through consortiums, technology coordinators should check to see what manufacturers are offering. Most manufacturers have academic licensing programs that make their software relatively inexpensive for educational organizations to use. Such purchasing programs may offer licensing of specific numbers of machines at a particular cost per machine; alternatively, all computers throughout a building or district can be covered by a *site license* for a specific price.

Whatever the choice of the organization, it is important for the technology coordinator to ensure that an appropriate number of licensed copies have been purchased for all programs to be installed on school or district equipment.

Once software is selected and installed on district workstations, one of the challenges for the technology coordinator

---

helpful hint

Home Use

Many software publishers offer district or building site licensees the right to extend their licenses to teachers for home use. Teachers who wish to work on school-related projects at home then enjoy the same software availability they have at school. This sort of licensing extension can be used for certain Microsoft products, such as Office. Licensing extension plans are available from a variety of other publishers as well. Technology coordinators should check with their software vendors or contact publishers to find out if such a program exists for the product they intend to purchase.

---

will be record keeping. Just as with equipment purchases, an accurate inventory of software installations should be established and carefully maintained.

The software versions that are installed in various locations must be kept track of to assure that a standard version is in use. This can be a very time-consuming task. Tracking the number of licenses installed in order to comply with current licensing agreements can also be quite challenging. A wide variety of software utilities can assist the technology coordinator with this task.

One example of such a utility is the Zenworks software program, which is available from Novell. This package provides a variety of tools to assist with the management of computers used by an organization. For software management, Zenworks provides reports on licenses currently in use on the network and also provides a detailed software inventory. This type of reporting can be critical in a large organization that is attempting to manage software installations in a variety of locations. More information about Zenworks features and capabilities can be found at www.novell.com/products/zenworks.

Equipment Maintenance and Upgrades

In addition to timely resolution of technical problems encountered by users, the technology coordinator must also be concerned with the regular maintenance and upgrading of equipment used by the organization. A regular, rigorous maintenance plan allows equipment to remain trouble-free and operational as long as possible. This planned maintenance should include the regular update of virus protection files, cleaning and repair of peripherals such as mice and printers, and periodic maintenance of the hard disk to ensure maximum performance.

Mission-critical hardware such as servers and other network equipment should receive special maintenance and support consideration. The purchase of extended warranties to cover such equipment, and service contracts to support it when problems do arise, is a wise use of technology-support dollars. Such equipment should also be protected with uninterruptible power supplies that include battery-run backup capabilities. Such equipment will protect sensitive hardware from fluctuations in power and provide emergency power should a general service failure occur.

It is also important for the organization to have a long-term plan for upgrading equipment. As the memory and processing demands of new software and peripherals increase, it is often necessary to replace a computer's *CPU* or increase its memory to make use of the most recent software or operating system. It is a good idea, consequently, to establish guidelines for the planned upgrade of equipment.

 Some districts may plan for equipment upgrade after a period of three years, with a maximum life expectancy of five years. Other districts may choose to phase out computers at the secondary level and then transfer them to the elementary level. Regardless, it is useful to have the procedures for the upgrade and maintenance of equipment clearly defined in the district technology plan. Clearly defined procedures for equipment upgrades and replacement help ensure that this process occurs smoothly at regular intervals and is built into the annual technology budget.

Equipment Recycling and Disposal

The technology coordinator must deal with computer equipment that has reached the end of its usable lifecycle. Obsolete and discarded electronic equipment is often referred to as *e-waste*. E-waste can contain a variety of hazards. Components, especially CRT monitors, contain a variety of environmental contaminants such as lead and mercury, in addition to a variety of other toxic elements. Examples of e-waste generated by a school district might be computers, monitors, DVD players, VCRs, and cell phones. Discarding such equipment through the normal waste system is no longer an appropriate action. Special planning and arrangements are often required for appropriately dealing with disposal of such equipment.

A total of 24 states have passed legislation that mandates the recycling and special disposal of e-waste, and a number of other states have begun to pass laws regulating this process. In many cases the cost of such programs is paid by the manufacturers, but laws differ depending on the state. It is important for the technology coordinator to research the laws of the state to see what procedures must be followed and what costs may be involved in the process.

The technology coordinator may also want to explore recycling programs offered by computer manufacturers. Apple Computer and Dell, for example, offer services that allow for the recycling and disposal of unwanted computer equipment. In some cases, manufacturers assist an organization in evaluating equipment for resale and may be able to help with data destruction to assure that no confidential records or important information is lost or stolen. Such services may be free, or charges may be incurred depending on the services required. The technology coordinator should work with computer vendors and recyclers to see what types of services are available and what the potential cost may be to the organization. Considering these costs up front, at the beginning of a purchase cycle, may make it easier for the organization to plan for equipment obsolescence, and then have the resources in place to safely and effectively deal with the disposal of equipment that is no longer needed.

Meeting IT Staffing Needs

Every technology coordinator faces the challenge of acquiring and maintaining a staff that can provide effective technical support services. During lean budget conditions, technology support positions may be identified as places where personnel costs can be reduced. It is important for the technology coordinator to establish necessary levels of technical support services and to provide effective arguments to leadership for why these service positions are necessary and should be maintained, even when budgets are tight.

School districts spend a considerable amount of funds developing technology infrastructure, establishing networks, and installing educational technology resources. As Lesisko & Wright (2007) point out: "staff should be in place for hardware, network, and infrastructure support." To make effective and efficient use of technology resources, technology coordinators must ensure that equipment works properly and that problems are addressed in a timely manner. The development of technology resources is an investment that must be attended to and supported in an ongoing fashion. "For technology to impact student learning, appropriate resources must be in place to support and maintain networks and equipment. Technical support is also essential so that all systems work 24/7" (Barnett, 2001).

Technical support is a critical requirement for successful use of technology in schools and classrooms. It is a sad fact that many districts do not allocate the necessary resources for districtwide technology support. When a district is unable to provide the necessary level of technology support personnel, service requests may take weeks to complete and may create major problems in continuity and the use of technology in the classroom. The technology coordinator must work with district administration to guarantee that adequate support personnel are available to ensure rapid responses and accurate problem resolutions. It is essential for the technology coordinator, along with other district planners, to determine ongoing funding sources for a technology plan, which in turn affords the necessary personnel to effectively support technology on a long term basis.

Grants

Grants have become a regular part of the funding equation for educational technology leaders. While grants should not be viewed as a routine component of the regular technology budget, they can provide useful dollars for exploring new technologies, funding innovative projects, and enhancing professional development opportunities. Grant applications often require considerable time and intense work and commitment from the technology coordinator, but they can also provide welcome additional resources.

Two basic types of grants are available to schools: entitlement grants and competitive grants. Entitlement grants are those funds allocated to schools and districts primarily on the basis of a formula. The formula is intended to distribute the available funds to districts based on an equitable funding method. Funding of entitlement grants is not competitive but is based on eligible student count and other data.

Examples of entitlement grants include Title I, Title VI, or Eisenhower funds. The purpose of entitlement grants is to provide funding to state and local educational agencies to help them implement educational programs. Entitlement grants provide funds mandated by law. Local educational agencies set up entitlement grant programs based on the criteria of the entitlement program. Appropriations are usually determined by formulas based on enrollment, high concentrations of low-income families, and other needs factors. To receive entitlement funding from a state or federal agency, local school districts must report a variety of data about their student population, for example, enrollment, participation in the free and reduced-fee lunch program, and so forth.

Competitive grants are programs in which the applicant designs a project that competes with other applications for funding. The agency that sponsors the grant program selects projects and determines grant amounts based on preestablished selection criteria. Some competitive grant programs are funded by state or federal education agencies. Other sources for competitive grant funds are programs sponsored by private foundations or businesses. While entitlement grants are usually based on financial need, competitive grants are most often awarded based on specific criteria specified by the funding source. Most competitive grant applications are evaluated on issues such as the potential benefit to the students, how well the project addresses an educational need, and the integrity of the project's objectives, planning, and budget.

While each grant is different, most grants tend to be made up of the same basic components: an executive summary, a statement of needs, the project's goals and objectives, a project narrative, and a budget for the project. The executive summary provides a clear overview of the project in a concise format. The statement of needs details the compelling reason for the project. The goals lay out the project's intended results. The objectives suggest ways to evaluate the success of the project. The project narrative provides a specific plan for what will happen and when. The project budget clearly explains, in concise

---

helpful hint

Grant Writing

Solomon (2001) provides some very useful pointers on things to do before beginning to write a grant:

- Have a solid idea and plenty of supporting details.

- Read the guidelines carefully and make sure the grant fits your needs.

- Involve others to build commitment to the project so that there is plenty of support to carry out the project, if funded.

- Make sure the funding will be sufficient for the project; look for matching funds from other sources if necessary.

- Make sure you have the commitment from administration to carry out the project.

- Read all the directions and follow them carefully.

---

terms, how the funding for the project will be spent.

Successful grant writing requires that the technology coordinator come up with a workable idea that fits the grant criteria, provide a project outline that will persuade the grant reader of the value of this idea, and list enough details to make it clear the project is doable.

As mentioned, developing successful grant applications is a time-consuming process. The first step in the process involves developing a grant concept that meets both the criteria of the grant and the need of the organization. Data must be gathered to support the organization's need. This data must provide information about how the grant project will support the need. When developing the grant concept, it is important that the technology coordinator communicate with, and gather support from, district staff and administration to ensure it will be possible to carry out the project. A funded project may be based on an outstanding concept, but if the staff and administration do not support the project, it will have little chance of being successful.

Once a grant concept has been selected and support for the project assured, the actual writing of the proposal can begin. A proposal usually starts with an executive summary, which is a brief summary of the entire grant proposal that gives the reader a general understanding of the project. As a first look, the executive summary provides information on the problem to be addressed, a summary of the project and how it will deal with the problem, and a summary of the funding requirements of the project. The executive summary is the part of the proposal that gets a grant reader's attention and creates interest in the project.

The executive summary is followed by a detailed statement of need. This statement provides the facts and figures that support the need, and it helps the reader understand the issues involved. This statement also ties the identified need to the mission and goals of the organization. For example, if the grant is intended to strengthen the use of technology in the learning process, the statement of need shows how the grant would support the district goals of integrating technology into instruction. While the statement of need must provide background and tie the project to the solution, it does not have to be long. Concise and persuasive writing will be more effective than a long and involved narrative.

The next section of the proposal is the project description. This section usually includes four subsections: objectives, methods, staffing/administration, and evaluation. Objectives are the measurable outcomes of the program. Your objectives must be specific, measurable, and achievable in a specified time period. The methods section describes the specific activities that will take place to achieve the objectives. You will need to devote a few sentences to discussing the number of staff, their qualifications, and specific assignments. An evaluation plan should not be considered only after the project is over; it should be built into the project. Including an evaluation plan in your proposal indicates that you take your objectives seriously and want to know how well you have achieved them.

Finally, a budget for the project must be prepared. The budget for your proposal may be as simple as a one-page statement of projected expenses or may require a more complex presentation. The budget is intended to help both you and the funding source understand how the money will be spent. For most projects, costs should be grouped into subcategories, which are selected to reflect the critical areas of expense.

You might divide your expense budget into personnel and nonpersonnel costs. Your personnel subcategories might include salaries, benefits, and consultants. Subcategories under nonpersonnel costs might include travel, equipment, and printing, with a dollar figure attached to each line.

Grants are all about meeting the needs of the organization: "Money by itself is not the answer; it is important to remember that you're there to meet the needs of the school" (Coburn, 1999). By taking the time to explore grant funding opportunities, working with others to develop the support needed to carry out a grant project, and crafting a winning grant application, the technology coordinator can secure the funding necessary to carry out a meaningful technology project.

Tech Leader Profile 10

Steve Taffee, Director of Technology

Steve Taffee is the director of technology for Castilleja School in Palo Alto, California. Castilleja School is a suburban school, and the only nonsectarian all-girls middle and high school in the San Francisco Bay Area. The school serves 415 girls in grades six through twelve with a faculty of 66 individuals. Steve has served as the director of technology for the past six years and reports to the head of school. He was originally trained as a high school English teacher, served as director of teacher education at North Dakota State University, and later joined the Minnesota Educational Computing Corporation (MECC). In addition to BS and MA degrees, Steve earned a PhD in curriculum and instruction.

Steve supervises a staff of three others who work in the technology department for the school. His main responsibilities are (1) planning and implementing instructional and operational technology initiatives; (2) hiring, supervising, and retaining technology staff; and (3) communicating with all constituent groups regarding school technology practices and issues. Steve identifies creating a shared vision and buy-in for technology with other administrators, faculty, and staff as his greatest challenge in being an effective technology leader. His tip for other technology leaders is "See the big picture, understand that your program is competing for limited resources, and make it a win–win proposition for all involved."

E-Rate Applications

Locating adequate funding to support a technology program is always a challenge for schools and districts. Technology coordinators can help bridge funding gaps by participating in the E-Rate program, which was established by the Federal Communications Commission and made available through the Schools and Libraries Division (SLD) of the Universal Service Administrative Company.

The E-Rate program was established as part of the Telecommunications Act of 1996 to improve telecommunications services in schools, libraries, and hospitals. By participating in this program, the technology coordinator can help the school or district improve its telephone and Internet connectivity, purchase computers and software, and provide additional training for teachers and staff.

The E-Rate program bridges funding gaps by offering schools discounts of 20% to 90% for telecommunications services they purchase or improvements they make to their network infrastructure. All schools can participate in the program by developing a technology plan, determining what services they currently use or wish to acquire, soliciting any necessary bids for those services, and awarding contracts based on the bids.

The technology coordinator begins the E-Rate funding process by filing Form 470. The technology coordinator uses this form to provide the description of services and required improvements. The number of free and reduced-fee lunches served by the school or district determines the amount of the discount. Those districts serving students with greater levels of need receive the highest discounts. Bids must be solicited to determine the actual cost of these services and improvements.

After bids have been solicited, final negotiations completed, and agreements made, the technology coordinator takes the second formal step in the process: filing Form 471, the Services Ordered Confirmation form. This form describes the actual costs of the services selected, determines the level of discount available to the district, and formally completes the first phase of the E-Rate application. Form 471 must be filed according to the deadline determined annually by the SLD.

When the E-Rate filing deadline has passed, the Schools and Libraries Division processes all Form 471 applications, determines the amount of funds requested across the nation, verifies applications, and decides the E-Rate awards for each applicant. All schools that apply within the eligibility window qualify for discounts on telecommunications services, such as basic telephone service, long-distance charges, and Internet access. Once these services have been provided to all applicants, any remaining funds are distributed to schools for network infrastructure improvements, which are referred to as internal connections, beginning with those schools in greatest need.

The Schools and Libraries Division implemented changes when considering applications for internal connections. Starting in funding year 2005, eligible entities were able to receive support for internal connections in only two out of every five funding years. The five-year period begins in any year in which an entity receives support for internal connections. This limitation does not apply to telecommunications and Internet access services.

All schools can benefit from the discounts on telecommunications services and Internet access. These services alone can total thousands of dollars for a school or district, and the discounts can allow technology coordinators to allocate additional funds to other technology projects.

When final decisions have been made on the discounts available to a district, an official Funding Commitment Decision letter is issued. This letter identifies the level of discount and the amount of funding available from each service provider identified on Form 471. Following the receipt of the funding letter, the district must file a Form 486, which acknowledges the receipt of services from the vendor and allows the district to officially begin receiving discounts or rebates on services.

In order to begin receiving the actual discounts on services, the district needs to work with service providers to determine the most appropriate method of receipt. Discounts may automatically be applied to monthly bills for services or received as a cash rebate. To receive cash payments, the district must, in conjunction with the service provider, complete Form 472, the Billed Entity Applicant Reimbursement (BEAR) form. This form identifies services that are received from a vendor and paid in full. Filing a BEAR form notifies the Schools and Libraries Division to issue a rebate to the vendor. The rebate will be passed on to the district in the form of a check.

While direct discount billing may be simpler for both the district and vendor, there may be situations in which the receipt of a rebate check is more appropriate and desirable. The technology coordinator should work with administration, business officials, and service providers to determine which method is most convenient and advantageous.

E-Rate Success

Following are 10 tips for success with the E-Rate program application process:

1. Begin thinking about E-Rate early. Deadlines always arrive at busy times, and the application process can take longer than expected.

2. Spend time researching the current cost of services used by the district. This may help identify new areas in which to apply for E-Rate funding.

3. Be familiar with the products and services eligible for discount.

4. When in doubt about something related to the E-Rate process, call the SLD Program Assistance Hotline for help, 1-888-203-8100, or visit their website for assistance, www.sl.universalservice.org.

5. Be sure to read directions carefully, fill in all required blanks on forms, and file forms by the deadlines.

6. Include E-Rate in the technology planning process to ensure compliance with all program requirements and certifications.

7. Keep copies of all forms submitted in case they are needed for reference or program audit.

8. If you disagree with a funding decision, file an appeal. It will take time for a decision, but there will be no penalty and the results may be to your advantage.

9. If necessary, hire an E-Rate consultant. These consultants offer management services and provide help with paperwork. They charge 5% to 8% of the discounts received and will take care of the entire application process. It is important to note that vendors of E-Rate services should not be allowed to complete E-Rate forms and other paperwork for a district. Such action is prohibited by SLD rules, and doing so is grounds for disqualification from the program.

10. Always budget fully for any services requested through the E-Rate program. Requests can be denied or funding reduced. If sufficient funds have not been budgeted, important services or projects can fail due to lack of funding.

ANSWERS TO

Essential Questions

1. What should the technology coordinator know about developing a comprehensive and successful technology plan?

    The technology coordinator must work with administration, staff, and community members to develop a comprehensive plan that will address all aspects of the technology program implemented in the district.

2. How can the technology coordinator assist administrators in creating and carrying out a sound technology budget?

    The technology coordinator must work with administrators, curriculum committees, and school constituencies to identify technology needs. Funds must be carefully allocated to support fixed costs, equipment purchases, maintenance and upgrades, and new initiatives.

3. How can the technology coordinator assist in evaluating the effectiveness of technology use in the school or district?

The technology coordinator should be familiar with resources and tools that can be used to assess technology use and integration. It is important to share evaluation results with stakeholders to guide ongoing planning efforts.

4. What must the technology coordinator do to ensure proper licensing of software?

By keeping an up-to-date inventory of equipment and software and working with teachers and schools to purchase the required licensing agreements, the technology coordinator can ensure that software programs are properly licensed and installed.

5. What must the technology coordinator do to make sure equipment is properly maintained, upgraded, and repaired as necessary?

The technology coordinator must work with the school or district administration to establish plans for the necessary maintenance and replacement of equipment. An established plan for regular equipment upgrades will maximize performance and minimize the chances of equipment failure. A system for reporting problems, answering questions, and providing needed assistance and repairs must be established. Creating a set of standard procedures for requesting services and repairs ensures that problems are documented in a systematic manner and that problems are resolved in a timely fashion. By implementing a standard reporting and tracking system for repair requests, it is also possible to gather data about departmental performance. This data can be used in a variety of ways for technology planning and staffing considerations.

6. What role should the technology coordinator play in the recycling and disposal of computer equipment?

The technology coordinator should be familiar with state laws regulating the proper disposal of e-waste. The technology coordinator should work with local, state, and national recycling and disposal programs to ensure that equipment is disposed of according to procedures that protect the environment and guarantee the appropriate destruction of data and confidential records.

7. **What can the technology coordinator do to assist the district in hiring the appropriate IT staff?**

   The technology coordinator must work with district administration to guarantee that adequate support personnel are available to resolve problems rapidly and accurately. This work includes identifying key positions to be filled, developing clear job descriptions and expectations, and hiring candidates with the appropriate skills for positions in hardware, network, and infrastructure support.

8. **What does the technology coordinator need to know about grant writing to locate and secure additional funding for technology projects?**

   By involving a variety of people in the planning process and constructing an effective grant application, the technology coordinator can help locate needed funds for innovative projects.

9. **What should the technology coordinator know about the E-Rate program and application process?**

   By understanding the various steps and forms involved in the E-Rate application process, the technology coordinator can help the district acquire discounts on products and services that will assist in the support of the district technology program.

Resources

Print Resources

Barnett, H. (2001). *Successful K–12 technology planning: Ten essential elements.* (ERIC Digest). Syracuse, NY: ERIC Clearinghouse on Information and Technology. (ERIC Document Reproduction Service No. ED457858)

Branzburg, J. (2001). How well is it working? *Technology and Learning, 21*(7), 24–35.

Coburn, J. (1999). Successful approaches to funding. *Technology and Learning, 19*(6), 54–58.

CoSN K–12 CTO Council. (2004). Essential skills of the K–12 CTO. *Learning & Leading with Technology, 32*(4), 40–45.

Espey, L. (2000). *Technology planning and technology integration: A case study.* San Diego, CA: Society of Information Technology and Teacher Education International Conference Proceedings. (ERIC Document Reproduction Service No. ED444467)

Fulton, D. (1998). *E-Rate: A resource guide for educators.* Syracuse, NY: ERIC Clearinghouse on Information and Technology. (ERIC Document Reproduction Service No. ED420307)

Heinecke, W., & Blasi, L. (1999). *New directions in the evaluation of the effectiveness of educational technology.* Washington, DC: The Secretary's Conference on Educational Technology Proceedings. (ERIC Document Reproduction Service No. ED452825)

Lesisko, L. (2005, March). *The K–12 technology coordinator.* Sarasota, FL: Paper presented at the annual meeting of the Eastern Educational Research Association March 2–5, 2005. (ERIC Document Reproduction Service No. ED490035)

Lesisko, L., & Wright, R. (2007, April). *School based leadership for instructional technology.* Chicago, IL: Paper presented at the Annual American Educational Research Association meeting April 9–13, 2007. (ERIC Document Reproduction Service No. ED497706)

New York State Education Department. (1996). *Guidelines for instructional technology planning and application.* Albany, NY: New York State Education Department Office of Facilities Planning. (ERIC Document Reproduction Service No. ED428510)

Salpeter, J. (2002). Accountability: Meeting the challenge with technology. *Technology and Learning, 22*(6), 20–30.

Solomon, G. (2001). Writing and winning grants. *Technology and Learning, 21*(11), 44–50.

Staihr, B., & Sheaff, K. (2001). *The success of the E-Rate in rural America.* Kansas City, MO: Federal Reserve Bank Center for the Study of Rural America. (ERIC Document Reproduction Service No. ED455082)

Online Resources

ALTEC ProfilerPro (technology surveys available):
www.profilerpro.com

Apple Recycling Program: www.apple.com/recycling

Dell Recycling:
http://content.dell.com/us/en/corp/dell-environment-recycling.aspx

District Technology Self-Assessment Form:
www.fno.org/techsurvey.html

Examples of Educational Technology Surveys from the U.S.
Department of Education: An Educator's Guide to Evaluating
the Use of Technology in Schools and Classrooms:
www2.ed.gov/pubs/EdTechGuide/appc.html

Index of Successful Grant Proposals:
http://k12grants.org/samples/samples_index.htm

Institutionalization of Technology in Schools Checklist: www.wmich.
edu/evalctr/archive_checklists/institutionalizationoftech.pdf

Integration of Technology Observation Instrument: www.west.asu.
edu/pt3/assessment/documents/ASUWObservation.pdf

National Center for Technology Planning: www.nctp.com

National Educational Technology Standards Project:
www.iste.org/standards

Office of Educational Technology: Grant Programs:
www2.ed.gov/about/offices/list/os/technology/edgrants.html

Technology Information Center for Administrative Leadership:
www.portical.org/matrix1.html

USAC Schools and Libraries E-Rate Site: www.sl.universalservice.org

U.S. Department of Education, Office of Educational Technology:
www2.ed.gov/about/offices/list/os/technology

appendix A

sample job descriptions

POSITION TITLE

Technology Coordinator

DEPARTMENT

Technology

REPORTS TO

Head of School

SUMMARY

The technology coordinator is responsible for setting and implementing the overall strategy and operations for the school's technology curriculum and its computer and telecommunications systems. The coordinator is also responsible for all administrative and interpersonal aspects of management for the Technology Department including budgeting, staff development, and employee performance.

job description 1 *(continued)*

ESSENTIAL DUTIES AND RESPONSIBILITIES

Academic Leadership

- Directs the development and ongoing assessment of the school's technology curriculum.

- Works cooperatively with faculty department heads to develop and support technology courses.

- Develops long-range staff development programs for technology.

- Oversees the Summer Technology Grant Program and other faculty and staff in-service programs for technology.

- Promotes technology as a field of study to the school's faculty and students.

- Serves as a member of the Academic Council and Leadership Council.

Strategic Planning

- Directs annual technology needs assessment and long-range planning.

- Co-chairs the Technology Committee.

- Anticipates technological developments and staff needs; proactively seeks and evaluates new technologies to ensure that the school is prepared for future technological advances.

Operations

- Creates and manages the school's technology budget; approves expenditures within budgetary spending guidelines.

- Works with appropriate staff to support their use of business computer systems.

- Leads the development, configuration, and testing of the master disk images for computer systems.

- Provides overall leadership for the school's website.

job description 1 *(continued)*

- Supervises the acquisition, installation, and disposal of computer hardware and software.

- Oversees the maintenance of telephone and voicemail systems.

- Maintains relationships with all third-party technology vendors.

- Assures that departmental processes and procedures are adequately documented.

Communications

- Seeks collaborative relationships between the school and major private industry executives and corporations.

- Represents the school at meetings on computer technology and education.

- Works with the development office to coordinate computer donation programs.

- Promotes the school technology programs through internal and external communication channels and publications.

EDUCATION AND EXPERIENCE REQUIREMENTS

Education

- Advanced degree in education, computer science or a related field, and/or equivalent combination of education and experience.

Skills and Knowledge

- Demonstrated ability to communicate effectively, both in writing and verbally, in an academic environment.

- Demonstrated ability to manage management tasks such as budgets, administrative forms, and purchasing of new equipment, software, and related materials required by the department.

job description 1 *(continued)*

- Demonstrated ability to manage personnel issues such as performance reviews, staff training, conflict resolution, promotions, staff leaves, and salary recommendations.

- Demonstrated high level of success in leading and motivating technical staff in a highly collaborative, dynamic environment.

PHYSICAL DEMANDS AND WORKING ENVIRONMENT

This job is performed in a multi-building school environment and computer lab setting.

BUSINESS EQUIPMENT, SYSTEMS, AND/OR TOOLS REQUIRED

This job requires the use of computers, software, and peripheral devices.

job description 2

POSITION TITLE

Coordinator of Technology

REPORTS TO

Assistant Superintendent for General Administration and with counsel from the Assistant Superintendent of Instruction

SUMMARY

Leads, directs, and administers technology for the District. Responsible for visioning, planning, selecting, and implementing instructional and administrative technology districtwide.

ESSENTIAL DUTIES AND RESPONSIBILITIES

- Sets vision and leads all technology initiatives for the district including students, teachers, administrators, and other stakeholders.

- Oversees the effective use of technology (voice, video, and data) districtwide, including personnel and equipment, network infrastructure, and budget.

- Supervises departmental staff; conducts performance and compensation appraisals for all districtwide information technology staff. Monitors internal training programs and coordinates common training needs and budget allowances. Develops and motivates all staff members in order to effectively achieve district objectives.

- Responsible for the overall technology security policy, including policies, procedures, and disaster recovery.

- Directs end-user support activities, including help desk services, hardware repair, network support, and administration and curriculum integration. Maintains all logs necessary to track repairs and support.

job description 2 *(continued)*

- Working with the Department of Instruction, provides input and resources for technology staff development needs for teachers.

- Assembles and communicates telecommunication plans, costs, and strategies.

- Oversees and coordinates new equipment installation and upgrades. Communicates regularly with hardware, software, and network vendors to correct problems, explore new technology, and determine the feasibility of system enhancements.

- Responsible for automating and enhancing efficiencies of district processes (imaging, online forms, and others).

- Maintains up-to-date knowledge of new technologies through literature, trade journals, membership in professional societies, conferences, etc.

- Plans and controls department budget including monitoring capital and operating expenses. Responsible for Universal Service Fund applications and other grant activities.

- Designs, develops, tests, and implements administrative systems for the district.

- 52 work weeks.

- Other duties as assigned.

EDUCATION AND EXPERIENCE REQUIREMENTS

- Bachelor's degree in instructional systems, management information systems, or related technology area required; master's degree preferred.

- Teaching certificate or experience working in school district technology setting, with increasing responsibilities preferred.

- Excellent communication skills required, both verbal and written. Ability to work with a variety of people at different levels, and an ability to develop consensus when appropriate.

job description 2 (continued)

- Proven leadership ability, including proven ability in problem solving and decision making, in both soft and technical situations required.

- Prior experience in a leadership role in an education or technical environment. Minimum of eight years of progressively more responsible work experience in a technology department preferred.

- Experience in recruiting, training, and supervising departmental staff required.

- Prior experience with instructional systems and the use of technology in the classroom required.

- Significant knowledge of networking and telecommunications concepts and theory required.

- Proven project management skills related to technology required.

- Knowledge of student management and school financial software required.

job description 3

POSITION TITLE

Coordinator of Technology

REPORTS TO

Superintendent

SUMMARY

Provide leadership and vision to the instructional program, and provide the design and implementation of administrative and instructional technology.

ESSENTIAL DUTIES AND RESPONSIBILITIES

- Develops and implements short- and long-range plans for the purchase and use of technology in an educational setting on the basis of identified needs.

- Designs and implements needs assessment tools for measuring the use and effectiveness of technology in the district.

- Coordinates technology aspects of district construction/ facilities projects.

- Initiates the development of, manages, and maintains the district's data gathering and data processing systems.

- Chairs the Instructional Technology Advisory Committee.

- Coordinates license agreements for software purchases.

- Maintains vendor relations.

- Maintains current knowledge of developments in the area of administrative and instructional technology.

- Secures instructional support materials related to educational technology.

job description 3 *(continued)*

- Assists in the training of certified and classified staff on the various operations of technology.

- Assists in locating special funding for hardware and software.

- Prepares grant proposals.

- Maintains liaison role and active involvement with curriculum personnel and curricular development at the state, regional, and national levels.

- Serves as a resource person to administrative personnel in improving individual teacher competencies.

- Works cooperatively with the director of school/community relations in disseminating information to the community.

- Evaluates assigned staff in accordance with board policies and administrative guidelines; conducts appropriate follow-up with notations to personnel files.

- Participates in decisions to hire, promote, demote, transfer, suspend, or discharge per board policies and administrative guidelines; makes specific recommendations regarding positions and personnel for which directly responsible.

- Assists in the development and management of the budget related to areas of responsibility.

- Attends board meetings as requested and assists with presentation of information and recommendations.

- Works cooperatively with building principals in the development and implementation of curriculum and technology.

- Provides information to the superintendent on all matters of relevance.

- Serves as a contributing member of the Administrative Leadership Team and other committees as assigned.

- Maintains professional growth through graduate work, professional organizations, seminars, and related professional literature.

- Performs other related duties as assigned.

job description 3 (continued)

EDUCATION AND EXPERIENCE REQUIREMENTS

Skills, Knowledge, and Abilities

- Ability to relate successfully with students, staff, parents, and community.
- Effective oral and written communication skills.
- Ability to handle diversity in an objective manner.
- Ability to work effectively through the committee process to accomplish goals.
- Expertise dealing with administrative and instructional technology.
- Knowledge of Department of Education curriculum requirements.
- Ability to identify needs and lead decision making about software and courseware.
- Knowledge and experience in assessing the effectiveness of the use of technology.
- Knowledge of WANS and LANS.
- Knowledge of budgeting procedures and management related to areas of responsibilities.
- Strong knowledge and skill in supervision and evaluation procedures.
- Ability to meet deadlines in a timely manner.
- Knowledge of good research procedures, ability to interpret data and make application to district's needs.
- Ability to anticipate problems and take preventive action.

Education, Certification/Licensure

- Bachelor's degree required.
- Teaching/administrative license preferred.
- Advanced degree/certification preferred.

job description 3 (continued)

Experience

- Technology leadership required.
- Teaching experience preferred.

SUPERVISION OF OTHERS

- Network engineer, lead PC technician, and data support specialist.
- Assist with the evaluation of others as requested.

PHYSICAL REQUIREMENTS

- Mobility as needed to visit all district buildings and classrooms.
- Must be able to drive a personal vehicle or to provide transportation suitable to accommodate responsibilities.
- Ability to occasionally lift equipment and supplies up to fifty pounds.

WORKING CONDITIONS

- Considerable in-district travel required.
- Frequent evening and Saturday work necessary.

TERMS OF EMPLOYMENT

- 12-month position.
- Per board policies and administrative guidelines.
- Performance evaluated per Administrator Performance Evaluation Handbook.

job description 4

POSITION TITLE

Technology Coordinator

REPORTS TO

Principal/Superintendent

ESSENTIAL DUTIES AND RESPONSIBILITIES

Technology Planning and School Leadership

- Prepare Technology Department budget.
- Purchase technology equipment, supplies, services.
- Supervise technology assistant, computer teacher, teacher technology leaders, and any student assistants.
- Chair and organize a Technology Committee.
- Prepare technology plan.
- Serve as the district's liaison to the Department of Education Office of Educational Technology.
- Assure compliance with state and federal mandates (such as email compliance).
- Participate as a member of the Leadership Team to form school policy.
- Participate in creation of the annual master schedule in conjunction with the Leadership Team and Guidance Departments.
- E-Rate.

Systems Administration

- Manage all servers at school and district level including server health, backups, and power management.
- Administer the network, switches, WAN, and Internet connection.

job description 4 *(continued)*

- Manage all staff and student user accounts.
- Establish systems/network policy for students and staff members.
- Implement group policies and centralized software deployments.
- Plan, evaluate, and purchase systems and software as needed.

Computer/Printer Support

- Troubleshoot and repair hardware and software issues (with the assistance of available Technology Department staff; contract for services when necessary).
- Purchase, install, maintain, and repair printers (or contract for repair services when necessary).
- Develop user guides and manuals.

Data Management

- Determine data management policy districtwide.
- Manage data integrity in all districtwide systems, including PowerSchool (student information system), NutriKids (food service system), Follett (library system), NWEA (assessment system), Active Directory (user account management system), Connect-ED (emergency communications system).

Communication

- Manage communication to parents, students, and community via the district's external website.
- Oversee production of school board and other public meeting videos and online posting of minutes (both tasks are usually contracted out).

Curriculum, Technology Integration, and Instructional Support

- Develop, implement, and revise computer technology curriculum in Grades PK–8.

job description 4 *(continued)*

- Implement ICT requirements per NH RSA ED 306.42.

- Provide technology resources to teachers, students, and parents, including assistance in modifying lesson plans to integrate technology, provision of technology resources to teachers/students, and communication of technology tools to students/parents.

- Assist Guidance Department in Internet safety curriculum.

- Develop and encourage multimedia (podcasting, video, and others) usage schoolwide in order to promote 21st-century skills in staff and students.

Assessment

- Serve as MAP Coordinator for NWEA testing, responsible for uploading student data, downloading test results, coordinating training, and coordinating distribution of data to teachers and administrators.

- When possible, collect assessment data in order to develop a long term archive of student information.

Training

- Provide documentation, user guides, manuals, and one-on-one training to teachers and staff members for district systems and software.

- Assist other members of the Leadership Team in providing training in district initiatives during teacher workdays, early releases, and small group meetings.

Other Duties as Requested by the Principal and/or Superintendent

job description 5

POSITION TITLE

Technology Coordinator

DEPARTMENT

Technology

REPORTS TO

District Director of Grants, Federal Programs, and Information Services

SUMMARY

Under supervision of the district director of grants, federal programs, and information services, coordinates district technology program—including networks, computers, and audiovisual media—and works as part of the district team to incorporate technology into the curriculum and instruction of Grades K–12. The position includes responsibilities such as working on committees; communicating and coordinating with disciplines, schools, grade levels, faculty, and staff; planning, designing, coordinating, and providing training; planning and facilitating technology equipment and supplies orders and implementing their use. Ensures smooth operation of the district's technology, educational access cable channel, satellite access, and distance learning.

QUALIFICATION REQUIREMENTS

To perform this job successfully, an individual must be able to perform each essential duty satisfactorily. The following requirements are representative of the knowledge, skill, and ability required. Reasonable accommodations may be made to enable individuals with disabilities to perform the essential functions.

job description 5 *(continued)*

ESSENTIAL DUTIES AND RESPONSIBILITIES

- Designs, oversees, maintains, and upgrades the district's network, components, and servers.

- Recommends, implements, and upgrades the district's network technology plan.

- Ensures regular and remote access to servers and the Internet.

- Implements the computer- and technology-education program of the district.

- Reviews and evaluates new educational and administrative software as it is developed.

- Works with committees to develop technology to meet instructional objectives.

- Coordinates workshops for the district's technology education program for the public.

- Coordinates distribution of computer software in the schools.

- Serves as a direct resource and consultant for faculty, staff, and students.

- Troubleshoots staff problems with technology and other equipment.

- Participates in development of district policies and procedures.

- Conducts research for the district and assists in disseminating findings.

- Networks with outside experts and imports worthwhile ideas and programs into the district.

- Coordinates follow-up to, and compliance with, state and national norms and mandates.

- Coordinates telecommunication services throughout the district, including television and distance learning.

- Prepares budget requests for technology areas.

- Other duties may be assigned.

job description 5 (continued)

COORDINATING RESPONSIBILITIES

Will coordinate computer technicians' daily activities.

EDUCATION AND EXPERIENCE

Bachelor's degree in education, business, or technology.
Experience in computer science and technology.

CERTIFICATES, LICENSES, REGISTRATIONS

No certification is required for this position.

job description 6

POSITION TITLE

Coordinator of Technology

SUMMARY

Provide an advanced level of technical expertise in technology planning, including developing standards and supporting the district's
personal computers, local area network, wide area networks, and
related technologies. Serve as primary resource for district personnel
in analyzing user problems related to computers, data communications, and platforms for current and future needs.

ESSENTIAL DUTIES AND RESPONSIBILITIES

Network Management

- Perform Novell network installations, documentation, and
  maintenance, such as adding new stations and providing
  users direct day-to-day assistance in solving network-related
  problems.

- Plan, implement, and manage wide area network and
  expansion of that network.

- Maintain and expand CPS connection to Internet through
  COIN and wide area network.

- Make strategic recommendations regarding network system
  design and implementation.

- Define network hardware and software requirements and
  perform network design and implementation.

- Design and aid in implementing data-cabling systems.

Computer Troubleshooting

- Consult with vendor personnel as part of the
  problem-determination/problem-resolution cycle.

- Research software problems and consult with vendors
  regarding resolution.

job description 6 (continued)

Acquisition Management

- Evaluate hardware and software configurations.

- Interface with vendors at a technical level and act as a technical resource for CPS staff members regarding network design and computer hardware.

- Write bid requests and specifications for purchases of new computers and data communications, and evaluate responses.

Education and Consulting

- Consult with staff on the utilization of telecommunications, computerized information retrieval, and software packages.

- Provide educational services, including onsite training and inservices that may be required for new and revised hardware and software systems.

Future Planning

- Research and make recommendations regarding future purchases, providing flexibility and design for technologies of tomorrow.

QUALIFICATIONS

Technical Skills Required

- Bachelor's degree in computer science, or an equivalent combination of education and experience from which comparable knowledge and abilities have been acquired.

- Broad background in installing and supporting Novell networks.

- Experience in troubleshooting, with a thorough understanding of PCs, networks, and data communications.

- Ability to closely track difficult problems, document them, and provide effective solutions.

job description 6 *(continued)*

Personal Skills Required

- Strong interpersonal and written communication skills, ability to develop positive working relationships with technical and nontechnical users and to maintain a positive approach when providing service to users, and ability to clearly and precisely document complex technical matters.

- Strong organizational skills and ability to effectively schedule multiple projects or tasks to meet simultaneous deadlines.

- Strong personal initiative and ability to work in a school environment without close supervision.

- Must be able to maintain positive approach despite conflicting deadlines, shifting priorities, and simultaneous work demands.

job description 7

POSITION TITLE

District Computer Coordinator

ORGANIZATIONAL RELATION

The district computer coordinator is accountable to the district media supervisor but works with the curriculum coordinator, staff-development coordinator, and media specialists to determine work priorities.

PRIMARY FUNCTION

To help teachers and media specialists integrate computer skills into the curriculum, and to help teachers obtain, learn, and use computer instructional materials to improve their instructional effectiveness.

ESSENTIAL DUTIES AND RESPONSIBILITIES

- In-servicing staff on computer skills integration.

- Training media specialists, computer lab aides, and library clerks.

- Previewing and recommending new equipment and software purchases.

- Developing software catalogs and informing staff of software.

- Tracking district software licenses and agreements and advising on building licensing.

- Working with media specialists and principals to help ensure district compliance with computer software copyright laws and policies.

- Working with the District Media Advisory Committee and District Staff Development Committee to develop list of staff technology competencies and inservice program.

job description 7 *(continued)*

EDUCATION AND EXPERIENCE

A master of arts degree from an accredited college or university, or the equivalent in educational technology, educational computing, or library media, and five years of successful classroom experience.

TIME REQUIREMENTS

Forty hours per week based on a 10.5-month contract. Hours may be flexible to accommodate inservices held outside the regular school day or school year.

appendix B

mini-grant application

<table>
<tr><td colspan="2">application for funding</td></tr>
</table>

Deadline for submission:

Time_____ Date_____

Return by email attachment to:

Contact person_____

PROJECT

Project Title _____

Name of grant contact _____

Contact's position:

☐ Teacher ☐ Administrator ☐ Counselor/Other

School_____

Project start/end dates_____

All projects must be completed by *(date)*_____

Estimated number of student participants_____

Estimated number of staff participants _____

Amount requested for this project_____

application for funding *(continued)*

BUDGET

Itemize your budget according to the following categories and briefly explain your planned spending on the attached spreadsheet template. Return the budget spreadsheet along with your grant application.

1. **Salaries/Stipends** (specify to whom and how much)

2. **Benefits** (must be included for all salaries and stipends; calculate at 12% of salary or stipend)

3. **Transportation** (list separately for student and faculty transportation)

4. **Equipment** (must be essential to the project)

5. **Supplies** (be as specific as possible)

6. **Other** (child care, other special needs, etc.)

7. Travel

PROJECT GOALS AND OBJECTIVES

_____

_____

PROJECT DESCRIPTION

Include information on the number of sessions involved and the number of contact hours:

_____

_____

Describe the products or accomplishments resulting from this project:

_____

_____

Describe how this project will be evaluated:

_____

_____

mini-grant budget

Name _____

School _____

Project Title _____

Category	Item	Description/Explanation	Amount
1	Salary		
1	Salary		
1	Stipend		
1	Stipend		
SALARY/STIPEND TOTAL:			
2	Benefits		
2	Benefits		
BENEFITS TOTAL:			
3	Transportation		
3	Transportation		
TRANSPORTATION TOTAL:			
4	Equipment		
4	Equipment		
4	Equipment		
EQUIPMENT TOTAL:			
5	Supplies		
5	Supplies		
SUPPLIES TOTAL:			
6	Other		
6	Other		
OTHER TOTAL:			
7	Travel		
7	Travel		
TRAVEL TOTAL:			
TOTAL BUDGET REQUESTED:			

nets·a

National Educational Technology Standards for Administrators (NETS·A)

All school administrators should be prepared to meet the following standards and performance indicators.

1. Visionary Leadership

Educational Administrators inspire and lead development and implementation of a shared vision for comprehensive integration of technology to promote excellence and support transformation throughout the organization. Educational Administrators:

a. inspire and facilitate among all stakeholders a shared vision of purposeful change that maximizes use of digital-age resources to meet and exceed learning goals, support effective instructional practice, and maximize performance of district and school leaders

b. engage in an ongoing process to develop, implement, and communicate technology-infused strategic plans aligned with a shared vision

c. advocate on local, state, and national levels for policies, programs, and funding to support implementation of a technology-infused vision and strategic plan

2. Digital-Age Learning Culture

Educational Administrators create, promote, and sustain a dynamic, digital-age learning culture that provides a rigorous, relevant, and engaging education for all students. Educational Administrators:

a. ensure instructional innovation focused on continuous improvement of digital-age learning

b. model and promote the frequent and effective use of technology for learning

c. provide learner-centered environments equipped with technology and learning resources to meet the individual, diverse needs of all learners

d. ensure effective practice in the study of technology and its infusion across the curriculum

e. promote and participate in local, national, and global learning communities that stimulate innovation, creativity, and digital-age collaboration

3. Excellence in Professional Practice

Educational Administrators promote an environment of professional learning and innovation that empowers educators to enhance student learning through the infusion of contemporary technologies and digital resources. Educational Administrators:

a. allocate time, resources, and access to ensure ongoing professional growth in technology fluency and integration

b. facilitate and participate in learning communities that stimulate, nurture, and support administrators, faculty, and staff in the study and use of technology

c. promote and model effective communication and collaboration among stakeholders using digital-age tools

    d. stay abreast of educational research and emerging trends regarding effective use of technology and encourage evaluation of new technologies for their potential to improve student learning

4. Systemic Improvement

Educational Administrators provide digital-age leadership and management to continuously improve the organization through the effective use of information and technology resources. Educational Administrators:

    a. lead purposeful change to maximize the achievement of learning goals through the appropriate use of technology and media-rich resources

    b. collaborate to establish metrics, collect and analyze data, interpret results, and share findings to improve staff performance and student learning

    c. recruit and retain highly competent personnel who use technology creatively and proficiently to advance academic and operational goals

    d. establish and leverage strategic partnerships to support systemic improvement

    e. establish and maintain a robust infrastructure for technology including integrated, interoperable technology systems to support management, operations, teaching, and learning

5. Digital Citizenship

Educational Administrators model and facilitate understanding of social, ethical, and legal issues and responsibilities related to an evolving digital culture. Educational Administrators:

    a. ensure equitable access to appropriate digital tools and resources to meet the needs of all learners

   b. promote, model, and establish policies for safe, legal, and ethical use of digital information and technology

   c. promote and model responsible social interactions related to the use of technology and information

   d. model and facilitate the development of a shared cultural understanding and involvement in global issues through the use of contemporary communication and collaboration tools

© 2012 International Society for Technology in Education (ISTE), www.iste.org. All rights reserved.

glossary

1-to-1 laptop initiative. Providing every student, teacher, and staff member with a portable laptop, notebook, or tablet PC for continuous use both in the classroom and at home. The intentions of such an initiative include improving the in-class educational experience, providing universal Internet access to disadvantaged homes, and building stronger connections between teacher and parent, as well as better school and community relations.

administrative computing. The computing done by an educational organization that includes such business tasks as budgeting, payroll, and purchasing. It also includes tasks such as management of human resources information and the processing of such student data as grades and other student records. These administrative tasks are usually carried out by professional office staff, and they are separate from the educational computing done by teachers and students.

adware. See *spyware.*

archive. A backup set of computer files that have been grouped and usually compressed to make available more storage space on a hard disk.

backup. Copies of files or databases that are placed in storage in case of equipment malfunction or other catastrophe. Backing up computer files is usually a regular part of the operation of servers and mainframe computers.

bid request. A formal or informal proceeding for obtaining the costs of specified goods or services. Formal bids are documents containing specifications detailing technical requirements for goods and services. Requests for bids are publicly advertised, and bids must be submitted in a sealed bid package or envelope. Formal bids are opened in public and read aloud.

blog. A shortened version of the term *web log*. A blog is a publicly accessible web page that serves as a personal journal or online diary written by an individual. Typically updated regularly (often daily), blogs often reflect the personality of the author. Bloggers write about a variety of different themes or topics, like a newspaper columnist, but with no specialized training required.

broadband. A type of high-speed data transmission in which the bandwidth is shared by more than one simultaneous signal. Such a transmission might include web pages (HTTP), file transfer (FTP), and video all on the same transmission line. The transmission of data over a fiber optic cable at a speed of many million bits per second would be referred to as broadband, as compared to a telephone modem operating at a rate of tens of thousands bits per second. Simply put, broadband is an Internet connection with a much larger capacity than dial-up.

CD. A compact disc designed to be read by a computer and intended to store computer data rather than audio music files.

cloning (a drive image). The copying of a complete hard drive as an image file so that the drive can be copied as a whole onto another computer. Cloning of hard drives makes possible the setting up of a single computer from which clones can be made and then installed on as many other machines as necessary.

cloud computing. A type of computing that relies on shared computing resources rather than local servers or devices to handle applications. This type of computing applies high-performance computing power to provide consumer-oriented applications such as financial portfolios or document creation and storage. Cloud computing networks rely on groups of servers, usually based on low-cost consumer PC technology, which spread data-processing chores across the server network. Cloud computing networks allow access to data and applications from any location with an Internet connection.

CPU. The central processing unit, or "brain," of the computer. This main unit does all the work of the computer and controls all the various systems that make up the computer.

cyberbullying. When students engage in bullying behavior using electronic means it is often referred to as online social cruelty or electronic bullying. Examples of this type of behavior can involve sending mean, vulgar, or threatening messages or images; posting sensitive, private information about another person; pretending to be someone else in order to make that person look bad, or intentionally excluding someone from an online group. A recent study showed that 18% of students in Grades 6–8 said they had been cyberbullied at least once in the last couple of months; and 6% said it had happened to them two or more times (Kowalski, Limber, & Agatston, 2007).

database. A collection of data organized in a standard format for easy access, management, and updating by a computer.

data processing. The conversion of raw data to a standard format that can be used by a computer and the subsequent processing—such as storing, updating, combining, rearranging, or printing—of this data by a computer.

digital citizenship. The norms of appropriate, responsible behavior with regard to technology use. Digital citizenship is a concept which helps teachers, technology leaders, and parents understand what students/children/technology users should know to use technology appropriately.

disaster recovery plan/procedures. Describes how an organization is to deal with potential disasters related to their technology infrastructure. A disaster recovery plan consists of the precautions taken so that the effects of a disaster will be minimized, and the organization will be able to either maintain or quickly resume mission-critical functions.

document imaging. The conversion of paper-based documents into computerized electronic images. A scanner is used to input documents into the system. The document-imaging system is designed to store images on a hard drive or optical disc for easy access of large amounts of data by one or more users.

drive image. A file that is an exact and complete image of an entire hard drive. The image contains information on the disk format and structure, a complete installation of the operating system, directories, and all files. A drive image can be used to make a complete copy of a hard drive on another computer or to restore a hard drive following an equipment failure.

DVD (digital videodisc). An optical disc designed for high-capacity storage that is often used for storage of video data files (such as a movie) or computer data.

educational technology. A term widely used to describe the use of technology tools and resources in an educational setting. Instructional technology refers to the use of the technology for teaching and learning.

email archive. In 2006, the U.S. Supreme Court revised rules regarding federal lawsuits called the Federal Rules of Civil Procedure. These rules require companies, government agencies, school districts, and generally any organization that might be sued in federal court to have systems for retrieving electronic data, such as email correspondence, if it is needed as evidence in a federal case.

email client. A program running on a computer that allows the user to send, receive, and organize electronic mail. An email client connects to a server-based mail account to check for new messages and send messages to others.

E-Rate. A government program that provides discounts to help most schools and libraries in the United States obtain affordable telecommunications and Internet access. This program includes three service categories: telecommunications services, Internet access, and internal connections of equipment. Discounts range from 20% to 90% of the costs of eligible services, depending on the level of financial need and the urban or rural status of the population served. Eligible schools, school districts, and libraries must apply for, and be awarded, the discounts on an annual basis, following the guidelines for the program.

ergonomics. An applied science concerned with the interactions of humans with the elements of a system they use. This includes the principles, data, and methods of design needed to optimize human well-being and overall system performance, particularly in a working or learning environment.

e-waste. E-waste is a popular, informal name for electronic products nearing the end of their useful life. Certain components of some electronic products contain materials that render them hazardous, depending on their condition and density. For instance, nonfunctioning CRTs (cathode ray tubes) from televisions and monitors are considered to be hazardous waste and must be disposed of properly.

fiber-optic line. See *high-speed communications line.*

help desk. A person or persons in an organization who serve as the first point of contact for users needing assistance and information in order to solve technical problems. Help desks are normally established to provide information-technology support, but they may be designed to support other functions of an organization as well.

high-speed communications line. A T1, T3, or fiber-optic line used for carrying voice or data communications signals. A T1 line can carry 24 digitized voice channels, or it can carry data at a rate of 1.544 megabits per second. A T3 line is a super-high-speed connection capable of transmitting data at a rate of 45 million bits per second. This represents a bandwidth equal to about 672 regular voice-grade telephone lines, which is wide enough to transmit full-motion real-time video, as well as very large databases, over a busy network. A T3 line is typically installed as a major networking artery for large corporations and universities with high-volume network traffic. Fiber-optic connections are essentially glass communications wire. Fiber-optic transmission lines can be used to support 30,000 times the traffic that can be carried on copper wires, which make up T1 or T3 lines.

hub. In network communications, a hub is a place of intersection where data arrives from one or more locations and is forwarded on in one or more directions. Hubs are quickly becoming obsolete as they are replaced by more useful and versatile network switches.

information management. Refers to the various stages of information processing—from creation and production to storage, retrieval, and dissemination—that is intended to improve the work flow of an organization. Prior to entering the management system, this information can be from internal and external sources and in a variety of formats.

infrastructure. In information technology and on the Internet, infrastructure is the physical hardware used to interconnect computers and users. Infrastructure includes the transmission media, including telephone lines, cable television lines, and satellites and antennas, and also the routers, aggregators, repeaters, and other devices that control transmission paths. Infrastructure also includes the software used to send, receive, and manage the signals that are transmitted.

instructional technology. Refers to hardware (such as personal computers, CDs, and multimedia, handheld learning devices) and software used in instructional programs. Also included are distance-learning activities, such as the Internet, videos, television, satellite, radio, cable, fiber optics, shortwave, microwave, and other related technologies.

interactive distance learning (IDL). A means of providing access to instructional programs for students who are separated by time and physical location from the instructor.

local area network (LAN). A computer network that covers a relatively small area. Most LANs cover a single building or a small group of buildings. A system of LANs can be connected over any distance through telephone lines and radio waves, creating a wide area network.

netbook. A small portable computing device, similar to a laptop computer, but smaller in size and with more limited features. What differentiates a netbook from a traditional laptop is its physical size and computing power. A netbook typically has a small display, ranging from 7 to 10 inches. It weighs less than 3 pounds, and has a keyboard that is reduced in size from 75% to 80% when compared to a standard keyboard.

network. A series of points or nodes interconnected by communication paths. In the case of computer networks, it is a variety of different equipment resources, each having a unique identification and serving a particular purpose, such as server, printer, switch, router, and so forth.

password. A sequence of characters typed during a connection sequence to verify that a computer user requesting access is authorized to use a system. Typically, users of a multi-user-protected single-user system claim a unique name, usually called a user ID. In order to verify that someone entering a user ID really is the person who's claimed that name, a second identification, the password, which is known only to that person and to the system itself, is entered by the user to gain access to the system.

patch panel. A hardware unit containing a set of port locations in a communications or other electronic system. In a network, a patch panel serves as a sort of static switchboard, using cables to connect computers within a local area network (LAN) and also to connect them outside to the Internet or another wide area network (WAN). A patch panel uses a network cable called a patch cord to create each interconnection.

podcast. This term originally referred to a digital recording of a radio-type broadcast or similar program, made available on the Internet for downloading, but has expanded to include video as well as audio. The word was originally derived from a combination of *iPod* (a trademarked device sold by Apple Computer) and *broadcasting*. Despite the source of the name, it has never been necessary to use an iPod, or any other form of portable media player, to make use of podcasts; the content can be accessed using any computer capable of playing media files.

print server. A dedicated electronic server that connects a printer to a network. This device enables users to print independently of the file server or a dedicated PC.

professional development. Professional training to improve and advance the knowledge, skills, and effectiveness of teachers for their own benefit and the benefit of their students.

repair ticket (trouble ticket). Keeping accurate records is vital to maintaining an organized, responsible IT support department. Help desks and computer technicians must sufficiently document the equipment they service and the work they perform. All help desks and support service offices should track the work done on every piece of hardware they service.

router. On the Internet, a router is an electronic device that determines the next network point to which a packet should be sent on its way toward its destination. The router is connected to at least two networks and decides which way to send each information packet based on its current understanding of the state of the networks it's connected to. A router is located at any gateway (where one network meets another), including each Internet point-of-presence. A router is often included as part of a network switch.

rubric. A scoring tool that lists the criteria for a piece of work, basically, "what counts." For example, purpose, organization, details, voice, and mechanics are often what count in a piece of writing. A rubric also articulates gradations of quality for each criterion, from excellent to poor. In essence, a rubric is an evaluation mechanism for rating the quality of a product based on particular criteria.

server. A specialized computer that is attached to a network and is used to provide the other computers in the network with such services as access to files or shared peripherals, or the routing of email.

site license. A license that gives permission to use a software package on more than one system. Site licenses are a means of providing a bulk rate to companies and schools that want to use software on many computers. Organizations are often able to negotiate special pricing when programs are used widely throughout the organization.

social media. A variety of web-based technologies and applications make up the social media that enable people to interact with one another online. Some examples of social media sites and applications include Facebook, YouTube, Delicious, Twitter, Digg, blogs, wikis, and other sites that have content based on participation and user-generated contributions.

social network (site or service). A website that enables users to create public profiles and form relationships with others. Social networks can be community-based websites, online discussions forums, chat rooms and other social spaces that exist online. A social network focuses on creating online communities of individuals who share interests, or who are interested in connecting with those with similar interests and activities. Most social networks are web based and provide a variety of ways for users to interact, such as email and instant messaging services.

software. A general term for the various kinds of programs used to operate computers and related devices.

spreadsheet. A computer program that allows the user to capture, display, and manipulate data that is arranged in rows and columns.

spyware. A technology that gathers information about a person or organization without their knowledge. Spyware usually refers to software that is covertly downloaded into someone's computer to secretly gather information about the user. It can be the relatively harmless gathering of generic information about websites visited, or it can be malicious, such as the collecting of passwords. A similar type of program is *adware,* a hidden software program that transmits user information to advertisers via the Internet. Both types of programs use up computer resources and network bandwidth and often cause problems for the computers on which they are running. Considerable time is spent by technical support staff who must remove this software from users' machines.

student information system. A software application used by educational organizations to manage student data. Student information systems provide capabilities for entering student test and other assessment scores through an electronic grade book, developing student schedules, tracking student attendance, and managing many other student-related data for easy access, backup, and analysis.

T1 line, T3 line. See *high-speed communications line.*

technology plan. A document that represents the very best thinking regarding technology use. In education, this thinking accumulates from a variety of stakeholders in a variety of environments—school buildings, school districts, communities, states, and so forth. Technology planning is used to determine ways in which the curriculum and the learning process can be strengthened through the use of technology, and the technology plan sets forth a detailed course to follow to achieve these goals.

Trojan horse. A program that does something users would not approve of if they knew about it. A virus is a particular type of Trojan horse, namely one that is able to spread to other programs. It is often a destructive program that masquerades as a benign one. For example, the user runs such a program, believing it has a useful function, when in fact it is designed to erase a hard drive.

troubleshooting. The process of systematically locating, diagnosing, and fixing problems concerning machinery, technical equipment, and other resources.

virus. A program or piece of code that is loaded onto your computer without your knowledge and runs against your wishes. Most viruses can replicate themselves and spread to other computers. All computer viruses are man-made. Anti-virus programs periodically check your computer system for the best known types of viruses.

VoIP. An acronym for Voice over Internet Protocol, a category of hardware and software that allows people to use the Internet as the medium for telephone calls by sending voice data in packets using IP rather than by traditional circuit transmissions of the public telephone network. One advantage of VoIP is that the telephone calls over the Internet do not incur a surcharge beyond what the user is paying for Internet access, much the same way that users do not pay for sending individual email messages over the Internet.

Web 2.0. This term describes a second generation of the World Wide Web that is focused on the ability to collaborate and share information online. Web 2.0 refers to the transition from static HTML web pages to a more dynamic WWW, organized and based on providing applications to users. Other features of Web 2.0 include open communication with communities of users and sharing of information. Blogs, wikis, and web-based services are seen as components of Web 2.0.

web browser. Computer programs (such as Firefox, Microsoft Internet Explorer, and Safari) that help you navigate the web and access text, graphics, hyperlinks, audio, video, and other multimedia. Browsers work by "translating" or "interpreting" hypertext markup language (HTML), the code embedded in web pages that tells them how to look.

wide area network (WAN). A network that connects several local area networks (LANs) over significant distances. WANs use technologies such as ISDN, frame relay, fiber-optic connections, or T1 leased lines to enable users on different LANs to communicate.

WiFi. This registered trademark term refers to a wireless networking technology that uses radio waves to provide wireless high-speed Internet and network connections. WiFi works with no physical wired connection between sender and receiver by using radio frequency (RF) technology. The cornerstone of any wireless network is an access point (AP). An access point broadcasts a wireless signal that computers can detect and connect to. In order to connect to an access point and join a wireless network, computers and devices must be equipped with special wireless network adapters.

wiki. A wiki is a collaborative website made up of the collective work of many authors. Similar to a blog, a wiki allows anyone to edit, delete, or modify content that has been placed on the wiki site using their browser, including the work of previous authors. A blog, in contrast, is typically authored by an individual and does not allow visitors to change the original posted material, only add comments to the original content. Wikis are often used to create collaborative websites, to power community websites, and for note taking.

worm. A self-contained computer program able to spread functional copies of itself to other computer systems, usually via network connections. Unlike viruses, worms do not need to attach themselves to a host program in order to do damage.

bibliography

Anderson, A. (2009). Can't we all just get along? *Learning & Leading with Technology, 37*(4), 21–23.

Anderson, R., & Dexter, S. (2000). *School technology leadership: Incidence and impact* (National Survey Report No. 6). Irvine, CA: Center for Research on Information Technology and Organizations. (ERIC Document Reproduction Service No. ED449786)

Bailey, G., & Ribble, M. (2007). *Digital citizenship in schools.* Eugene, OR: International Society for Technology in Education (ISTE).

Bakia, M., Yang, E., & Mitchell, K. (2008). *National educational technology trends study: Local-level data summary.* Washington, DC: U.S. Department of Education Office of Planning, Evaluation and Policy Development Policy and Program Studies Service. (ERIC Document Reproduction Service No. ED504192)

Barnett, H. (2001). *Successful K–12 technology planning: Ten essential elements* (ERIC Digest). Syracuse, NY: ERIC Clearinghouse on Information and Technology. (ERIC Document Reproduction Service No. ED457858)

Bateman, B. (2001). Maximizing your hardware investment. *Technology and Learning, 22*(3), 10–12.

Bateman, B. (2002). Installation made simple. *Technology and Learning, 22*(8), 46–48.

Baylor, A. L., & Ritchie, D. (2002). What factors facilitate teacher skill, teacher morale, and perceived student learning in technology-using classrooms? *Computers and Education, 39*(4), 395–414.

Borja, R. (2006). Technology upgrades prompt schools to go wireless. *Education Week, 26*(9), 10–11.

Branzburg, J. (2001). How well is it working? *Technology and Learning, 21*(7), 24–35.

Breiner, B. (2009). Creating tech wizards. *Learning & Leading with Technology, 36*(7), 24–27.

Brown, R. (1999). *Serving six institutions: A history of administrative computing at the Associated Colleges of Central Kansas.* McPherson, KS: Associated Colleges of Central Kansas. (ERIC Document Reproduction Service No. ED444414)

Bull, G., & Ferster, B. (2006). Ubiquitous computing in a web 2.0 world. *Learning & Leading with Technology, 33*(4), 9–11.

Bushweller, K. (1996). How mighty is your wizard? *The American School Board Journal, 183*(5), a14–a16.

Byrom, E. (2001). *Factors influencing the effective use of technology for teaching and learning.* Retrieved December 12, 2001, from www.seirtec.org/publications/lessons.pdf

Carter, D. S., Kelly, P., & Connors, M. (1996). *Implementing an instructional information management system in a catholic secondary school.* Paper presented at the National Conference of the Australian College of Education, Perth, Australia. (ERIC Document Reproduction Service No. ED413632)

Carter, K. (2000). Staffing up for technology support. *Technology and Learning, 20*(8), 26–33.

Cavanaugh, C., Barbour, M., & Clark, T. (2009). Research and practice in K–12 online learning: A review of open access literature. *International Review of Research in Open and Distance Learning, 10*(1). (ERIC Document Reproduction Service No. EJ831713)

CEO Forum on Education and Technology. (1997). *School technology and readiness reports: From pillars to progress.* Available from www.eric.ed.gov/ERICWebPortal/recordDetail?accno=ED416819

Christensen, R. (2001). Wiring the schools: South Dakota does it right. *Tech Trends, 45*(3), 18–20.

Clausen, M., Britten, J., & Ring, G. (2008). Envisioning effective laptop initiatives. *Learning & Leading with Technology, 36*(2), 19–22.

Coburn, J. (1999). Successful approaches to funding. *Technology and Learning, 19*(6), 54–58.

Conley, K. (Ed.). (2007). Student information systems buyer's guide. *Learning & Leading with Technology, 34*(4), 40–41.

CoSN K–12 CTO Council. (2004). Essential skills of the K–12 CTO. *Learning & Leading with Technology, 32*(4), 40–45.

Davis, M. (2007). Revised federal archiving rules raise legal, logistical challenges. *Education Week Digital Directions, 1*(3), 12–15.

Davis, M. (2009). Districts dial into the internet to modernize phone systems. *Education Week Digital Directions, 2*(3), 18–21.

Dietrich, D. (2003). How to obtain E-Rate funding. *School Business Affairs, 69*(4), 33–34.

Donovan, L., Hartley, K., & Strudler, N. (2007). Teacher concerns during initial implementation of a one-to-one laptop initiative at the middle school level. *Journal of Research in Technology and Education, 39*(3), 263–286.

Durost, R. A. (1994). Integrating computer technology: Planning, training, and support. *NASSP Bulletin, 78*(1), 49–54.

Earle, R. (2002). The integration of instructional technology into public education: Promises and challenges. *Educational Technology, 41*(1), 5–13.

Espey, L. (2000). *Technology planning and technology integration: A case study.* San Diego, CA: Society of Information Technology and Teacher Education International Conference Proceedings. (ERIC Document Reproduction Service No. ED444467)

Farmer, L. S. (2001). Managing the hard stuff: Technology. *Library Talk, 14*(4), 6–9.

Foa, L., Schwab, R., & Johnson, M. (1996). Upgrading school technology. *Education Week, 15*(32), 40, 52.

Fonesca, B. (2007) E-discovery rules add summer IT work for schools. Computerworld. Retrieved June 20, 2010, from www.computerworld.com/s/article/print/9024018

Fulton, D. (1998). *E-Rate: A resource guide for educators.* Syracuse, NY: ERIC Clearinghouse on Information and Technology. (ERIC Document Reproduction Service No. ED420307)

Gallagher, L., Means, B., & Padilla, C. (2008). *Teachers' use of student data systems to improve instruction: 2005 to 2007.* Report prepared for the U.S. Department of Education. (ERIC Document Reproduction Service No. ED504214)

Gray, L., Thomas, N., & Lewis, L. (2010). *Educational technology in U.S. public schools: Fall 2008* (NCES 2010–034). U.S. Department of Education, National Center for Education Statistics. Washington, DC: U.S. Government Printing Office. Retrieved May 15, 2010, from http://nces.ed.gov/pubsearch/pubsinfo.asp?pubid=2010034

Grohe, B., & Levinson, E. (2002). Managing technology is different. *Converge, 5*(1), 42–43.

Hallman, T. (1995). *Getting everyone into the tent.* Association of Small Computer Users in Education Conference Proceedings, Myrtle Beach, SC. (ERIC Document Reproduction Service No. ED387098)

Hannay, M., & Newvine, T. (2006). Perceptions of distance learning: A comparison of online and traditional learning. *MERLOT Journal of Online Learning and Teaching, 2*(1). Retrieved from http://jolt.merlot.org/documents/MS05011.pdf

Hardman, J., & Carpenter, D. (2007). Breathing fire into web 2.0. *Learning & Leading with Technology, 34*(5), 18–21.

Hardy, L. (2003). Information, please. *American School Board Journal, 190*(7), 20–22.

Harrington-Leuker, D. (2001). *New networks, old problems: Technology in urban schools.* Washington, DC: Education Writers Association Special Report. (ERIC Document Reproduction Service No. ED456188)

Heinecke, W., & Blasi, L. (1999). *New directions in the evaluation of the effectiveness of educational technology.* Washington, DC: The Secretary's Conference on Educational Technology Proceedings. (ERIC Document Reproduction Service No. ED452825)

Hoffman, B. (1996). Managing the information revolution: Planning the integration of school technology. *NASSP Bulletin, 80*(2), 89–98.

Hoffman, R. (2002). Strategic planning: Lessons learned from a "big-business" district. *Technology and Learning, 22*(10), 26–38.

Holland, L., & Moore-Steward, T. (2000). A different divide: Preparing tech savvy leaders. *Leadership, 30*(1), 6–10.

House, J. E. (1989). *The impact of personal computing technology on the educational administration knowledge base.* Education Writers Association Special Report, Washington, DC. (ERIC Document Reproduction Service No. ED387895)

Hovenic, G. (1997). *Log on to the future: One school's success story.* Des Moines, IA: Iowa State Department of Education. (ERIC Document Reproduction Service No. ED419518)

Institute of Education Sciences National Center for Education Statistics. (2000). *Teacher use of computers and the Internet in public schools.* Retrieved May 20, 2000, from www.nces.ed.gov/pubsearch/pubsinfo. asp?pubid=2000090

Jensen, D. (2000). Creating technology infrastructures in a rural school district: A partnership approach. In S. DeWees & P. Hammer (Eds.), *Improving rural school facilities* (pp. 57–69). Collected papers presented at the National Working Conference on Improving Rural School Facilities, Kansas City, MO. (ERIC Document Reproduction Service No. ED445859)

Jewell, M. (1999). The art and craft of technology leadership. *Learning & Leading with Technology, 26*(4), 46–47.

Johnson, L., Smith, R., Levine, A., & Haywood, K. (2010). *The 2010 Horizon Report: K–12 Edition.* Austin, TX: The New Media Consortium. Retrieved May 23, 2010, from http://wp.nmc.org/horizon-k12-2010

Joseph, R., & Reigeluth, C. (2002). Beyond technology integration: The case for technology transformation. *Educational Technology, 42*(4), 9–13.

Klein, J. (2008). Social networking for the K–12 set. *Learning & Leading with Technology, 35*(5), 12–16.

Kowalski, R. M., Limber, S. P., & Agatston, P. W. (2007). Electronic bullying among middle school students. *Journal of Adolescent Health, 41,* S22–S30. Retrieved June 22, 2010 from www.isb.sccoe.org/depts/csh/docs/Mar2011/ Elec.Bullying.Middle.School.pdf

Kranz, M. (2002). Networking systems and equipment. *School Planning and Management, 41*(5), 32–36.

Lamont, B. (1996). *A guide to networking a K–12 school district.* (Unpublished master's thesis). University of Illinois, Urbana-Champaign.

Lesisko, L. (2005, March). *The K–12 technology coordinator.* Sarasota, FL: Paper presented at the annual meeting of the Eastern Educational Research Association March 2–5, 2005. (ERIC Document Reproduction Service No. ED490035)

Lesisko, L., & Wright, R. (2007, April). *School based leadership for instructional technology.* Chicago, IL: Paper presented at the Annual American Educational Research Association meeting April 9–13, 2007. (ERIC Document Reproduction Service No. ED497706)

Maddux, C. (2002). Information technology in education: The critical lack of principled leadership. *Educational Technology, 42*(3), 41–50.

Manzo, K. (2010). Digital innovation outpaces E-Rate policies. *Education Week, 29*(20) 1, 16.

Marcovitz, D. M. (1998). *Supporting technology in schools: The roles of computer coordinators.* Washington, DC: Society for Information Technology and Teacher Education Conference Proceedings. (ERIC Document Reproduction Service No. ED421150)

McClure, P. A., Smith, J. W., & Sitko, T. D. (1997). *The crisis in information technology support: Has our current model reached its limit?* Boulder, CO: Association for Managing and Using Information Resources in Higher Education CAUSE Paper Series No. 16. (ERIC Document Reproduction Service No. ED403837)

McGillivray, K. (1999). The tool kit: An innovative approach to technology integration in networked schools. *Learning & Leading with Technology, 26*(5), 45–49.

Miller, S., & Brenner, D. (2002). *Regional decision-making practices in technology diffusion.* Paper presented at the annual meeting of the Kentucky Teaching and Learning Conference, Louisville, KY. (ERIC Document Reproduction Service No. ED481099)

Moursund, D. (1992). *The technology coordinator.* Eugene, OR: International Society for Technology in Education (ISTE).

Murray, B. (2001). Tech support: More for less. *Technology and Learning, 22*(4), 40–44.

New Mexico State Department of Education. (1995). *Educational technology institute report.* Santa Fe, NM: Author. (ERIC Document Reproduction Service No. ED460673)

New York State Education Department. (1996). *Guidelines for instructional technology planning and application.* Albany, NY: New York State Education Department Office of Facilities Planning. (ERIC Document Reproduction Service No. ED428510)

Ngoma, S. (2009). *An exploration of the effectiveness of SIS in managing student performance.* (ERIC Document Reproduction Service No. ED507625)

Ogle, T., Branch, M., Canada, B., Christmas, O., Clement, J., Fillion, J., et al. (2002). *Technology in schools: Suggestions, tools and guidelines for assessing technology in elementary and secondary education* (Report No. NCES-2003-313). Washington, DC: National Center for Education Statistics. (ERIC Document Reproduction Service No. ED474409)

Owens, A. (2009). Do your teachers need a personal trainer? *Learning & Leading with Technology, 36*(8), 14–17.

Palmer, S. (1997). *Leadership styles and problem solving: de Bono's "Six Hats."* Retrieved July 2, 2001, from www.deakin.edu.au/~spalm/srp70733.html

Peterman, L., McGillivray, K., & Frantz, J. (1998). Professional development: From reports to reality. *LNT Perspectives.* Retrieved November 11, 2001, from www.edc.org/LNT/news/Issue6/feature.htm

Quinones, S., Kirshstein, R., Loy, N. (1998). *An educator's guide to evaluating the use of technology in schools and classrooms* (Report No. ORAD-1999-1200). Washington, DC; Office of Educational Research and Improvement. (ERIC Document Reproduction Service No. ED425740)

Reilly, R. (1999). The technology coordinator: Curriculum leader or electronic janitor? *Multimedia Schools, 6*(3). Retrieved May 24, 2000, from www.umass.edu/ednet/janitor.html

Ribble, M. (2011). *Digital citizenship in schools* (2nd ed). Eugene, OR: International Society for Technology in Education (ISTE).

Rice, K. L. (2006). A comprehensive look at distance education in the K–12 context. *Journal of Research on Technology in Education, 38*(4), 425–448.

Ritchie, D. (1996). The administrative role in the integration of technology. *NASSP Bulletin, 80*(2), 42–51.

Rodriguez, J. (1997). Building an adaptive information system. *School Administrator, 54*(4), 22–25.

Rogers, A. (1996). Living in the global village. *Electronic Learning, 13*(8), 28–29.

Salpeter, J. (2002). Accountability: Meeting the challenge with technology. *Technology and Learning, 22*(6), 20–30.

Solomon, G. (2001). Writing and winning grants. *Technology and Learning, 21*(11), 44–50.

Son, T. (1998). *Network technology based application.* Portland, OR: Northwest Regional Educational Lab. (ERIC Document Reproduction Service No. ED417707)

Staihr, B., & Sheaff, K. (2001). *The success of the E-Rate in rural America.* Kansas City, MO: Federal Reserve Bank Center for the Study of Rural America. (ERIC Document Reproduction Service No. ED455082)

U.S. Department of Education. (1998). *An educator's guide to evaluating the use of technology in schools and classrooms.* (ERIC Document Reproduction Service No. ED425740)

U.S. Department of Education. (2000a). *e-Learning: Putting a world-class education at the fingertips of all children.* Retrieved November 22, 2001, from www2.ed.gov/about/offices/list/os/technology/reports/e-learning.pdf

U.S. Department of Education. (2000b). *Falling through the net: Toward digital inclusion.* Retrieved December 13, 2001, from http://search.ntia.doc.gov/pdf/fttn00.pdf

U.S. Department of Education. (2000c). *The power of the internet for learning: Moving from promise to practice.* Retrieved December 20, 2001, from www2.ed.gov/offices/AC/WBEC/FinalReport

U.S. Department of Education. (2010). *National educational technology plan 2010.* Retrieved June 22, 2010, from www.ed.gov/technology/netp-2010

U.S. Department of Education National Center for Education Statistics. (2000). *Teachers' use of computers and the Internet in public schools.* Retrieved May 20, 2000 from http://nces.ed.gov/pubsearch/pubsinfo. asp?pubid=2000090

Wasser, J. (1996). Navigating schools past the technology on-ramp. *Hands-On! 19*(2) 14–16. Retrieved November 11, 2001, from www.terc.edu/handson/f96/navigating.html

Wasser, J., & McNamara, E. (1998). *Professional development and full school technology integration.* Hanau Model Schools Partnership Research Brief No. 5. Cambridge, MA: TERC.

Weston, M., & Bain, A. (2010). The end of techno-critique: The naked truth about 1:1 laptop initiatives and educational change. *The Journal of Technology, Learning, and Assessment, 9*(6). Retrieved June 11, 2010, from http://escholarship.bc.edu/jtla/vol9/6

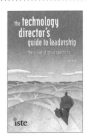
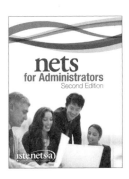

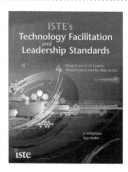